THE NEWPORT DOCKS & RAILWAY COMPANY

ALEXANDRA (NEWPORT & SOUTH WALES) DOCKS
AND
RAILWAY COMPANY,
NEWPORT MON.

A GWR map of Newport Docks, edition of 1934. *Courtesy Mr D. C. Sims, Newport Harbour Commissioners Office*

THE NEWPORT DOCKS & RAILWAY COMPANY

A portrait of the Alexandra (Newport & South Wales) Docks & Railway, and the Pontypridd, Caerphilly & Newport Railway

John Hutton

·MARITIME HERITAGE·
from
The NOSTALGIA Collection

I dedicate this book to my dear wife Linda,
and to Alun and Val Powell for their friendship over many years.

First published in 1996
This updated edition first published 2002

British Library Cataloguing in Publication Data

A catalogue record for this book is available from the British Library

ISBN 1 85794 163 2

Silver Link Publishing Ltd
The Trundle
Ringstead Road
Great Addington
Kettering
Northants NN14 4BW

Tel/Fax: 01536 330588
email: sales@nostalgiacollection.com
Website: www.nostalgiacollection.com

Printed and bound in Great Britain

SLP

A Silver Link book
from
The NOSTALGIA *Collection*

40

No. 7916 C.   N.L. 7817.

Certificate of Incorporation

OF THE

NEWPORT (ALEXANDRA) DOCK

COMPANY LIMITED.

I hereby certify that the Newport (Alexandra) Dock Company
Limited is this day incorporated under the Companies' Act, 1862,
and that this Company is Limited.

Given under my hand at London, this Sixteenth day of
December, One thousand eight hundred and seventy-three.

. E. C. CURZON,
Registrar of Joint Stock Companies.

Fee £28 15s.

Certificate of Incorporation of the Alexandra (Newport) Dock Company Ltd. *Courtesy Newport Public Library*

CONTENTS

ALEXANDRA (NEWPORT & SOUTH WALES) DOCKS & RAILWAY COMPANY

Showing Direct Communication by

The Company's Own Line (marked red)

between

The Merthyr, Aberdare and Rhondda Valleys

and

NEWPORT DOCKS

COAL FROM THE COLLIERIES INDICATED CAN BE BROUGHT TO NEWPORT AT AS CHEAP A COST IN RAILWAY CARRIAGE AND AS QUICKLY AS TO ANY NEIGHBOURING PORT.

The ss. "CLUMBER HALL" loading Rails from Dowlais at Alexandra Docks, Newport. (5035 tons) for India.

GLAMORGANSHIRE COLLIERIES AND NEWPORT ALEXANDRA DOCKS.

An ANDR Company map of the Glamorganshire Collieries and the PC&N line to Newport, November 1907. *Courtesy Cardiff Public Library*

INTRODUCTION

The Alexandra Docks at Newport was the brainchild of a group of influential businessmen who realised that the Old Town Docks there were fast becoming congested with the increase in water and inland traffic. On the instigation of the First Lord Tredegar, a movement was started towards the building of separate and larger docks. Eventually, after many months of negotiation, the Alexandra (Newport) Dock Company was born, incorporated by an Act of Parliament on 6 July 1865. The name Alexandra was taken from the marriage of His Royal Highness the Prince of Wales (later to become King Edward VII) to Her Royal Highness Princess Alexandra of Denmark in 1863.

Almost immediately work went ahead to excavate the area that would be known as the North Docks. Due to financial problems, however, this work did not go as quickly as had been planned, so it was not until 10 April 1875 that the North Dock and Lock was officially opened. In its first year the total imports and exports handled amounted to a total of 296,927 tons. By 1881 this total was 2½ million tons.

By the Act of Parliament of 1882 taking effect on 18 August, the two dock companies, the Alexandra (Newport) Dock Company and the Newport Dock Company, were amalgamated to become the Alexandra (Newport & South Wales) Docks & Railway Company (ANDR). On 1 January 1884 the ANDR also took over control of the Old Town Docks.

To tap into the rich coalfields of the Rhondda and Cynon Valleys and bring the coal to the Alexandra Docks, the Second Lord Tredegar, along with other members of the board, decided to construct and finance a railway line that would start at the market town of Pontypridd, via a junction with the Taff Vale Railway Company station there. This would then head eastwards to Caerphilly, and from there it would eventually reach the Alexandra Docks, the idea being to divert part of the tremendous amount of coal and iron traffic that otherwise would have found its way to the coal staithes of the Marquis of Bute Docks at Cardiff.

This line, to be known as the Pontypridd, Caerphilly & Newport Railway Company (PC&N), was incorporated by an Act of Parliament on 8 August 1878, but it was to be many years before the line was completed and able to carry mineral traffic, and later still for the carrying of passengers. Built to double-line width, it crossed the River Taff at Pontypridd, then followed the Glamorganshire Canal for a short distance before heading eastwards to join the Rhymney Railway at Penrhos Junction, using that company's line into Caerphilly station. After leaving Caerphilly the ANDR used the line of the Brecon & Merthyr Railway, running along that company's metals to Bassaleg Junction. From there the ANDR used the Great Western Railway Company lines for a short distance before reaching Newport and its own line leading into the internal system of the Alexandra Docks. This rather complicated journey was made all the more interesting by the fact that most of the rolling-stock used by the ANDR was former GWR stock, while the engines were driven for a number of years by drivers of the Taff Vale Railway.

Covering a total distance of just over 23 miles from the town of Pontypridd to the docks at Newport, there were also extensive sidings in use along the line and numerous lines inside the Alexandra Dock complex, so it is no wonder that by 1922 there were over 100 miles of track in use.

On 25 March 1922 the Alexandra (Newport & South Wales) Docks & Railway Company was amalgamated into the Great Western Railway Docks Department, passing into British Railways hands on nationalisation in 1948. In 1982 the docks became part of the Associated British Ports group, and today can be described as an all-purpose port; although it does still handle traditional cargoes, it also handles vehicles, general cargo, fruit, machinery and timber. Equipped to handle vessels of up to 40,000 tons deadweight in a combined water area of some 125 acres, it is indeed a modern port and an important part of the ABP operation.

I hope that this book will give all railway and maritime enthusiasts and historians a large yet varied subject to read and enjoy.

The new edition

This new edition, updating the history of Newport Docks with the changes of the last six years, was a task that I welcomed, for I have come to think of these docks with the same feelings that one has when seeing an old friend once again.

When Bill Clinton became President of the United States, there was an upsurge in the American economy, resulting in the price of Canadian timber increasing by about 80 per cent. The United Kingdom could not afford these inflated prices, but at the same time the Swedish krona was devalued by 20 per cent, which resulted in the majority of UK timber imports coming from the Baltic area via East Coast ports. Although very recently Newport Docks has subsequently regained some of its market share, to replace the lost timber market Associated British Ports looked into the handling of alternative cargoes. This led to an agreement with two major companies to import the raw materials needed to make animal feed, such as palm kernel, sunflower seeds, soya beans, etc; the company also invested in two new bulk cargo sheds, together with hopper and loading shovels.

Since 1980 Jamaica Producers Marketing Company had imported weekly shipments of bananas and other fresh fruit produce, mainly from the island of Jamaica and Costa Rica, but quite recently the company left Newport Docks, transferring its operations to the South Coast, thus saving their vessels sailing time and fuel costs en route to the Continent.

On the plus side, over the past two years there has been a significant increase in imported steel from Brazil and the Far East, thus increasing employment in the docks; to cover this increase and the movement of traffic, Associated British Ports has invested heavily in new shed accommodation, nine of which have been built so far, with two more awaiting construction in 2002.

The Colt Motor Company contract for the storage of motor cars and vans was lost to Avonmouth Docks many years ago, and has left a large area of unoccupied dockland space; however, new leases are always available, so it is hoped that a new motor storage contract will not be far off.

1. THE NORTH DOCK

The North Lock (Act of 1865)

Immediately after the opening speeches were made on 10 April 1875, a button was pressed and the huge dock gates opened electronically. In that first year 982 vessels would pass through the lock, which was some 350 feet in length and 65 feet wide, with access gained via the River Usk. Trade through the lock steadily increased, so much that eventually a new entrance lock had to be opened in 1914. As a result trade in the docks via the North Lock gradually decreased, and in 1919 this access was closed and converted into a dry dock (now known as Messrs C. H. Bailey's Dry Dock). By 1934 this dry dock was extended to 415 feet in length, and the lock entrance to 60 feet wide. Today the dry dock is part of the Bristol Channel Ship Repairs Limited, under the ownership of Messrs C. H. Bailey Group plc; with a length of 454 feet and a width of 64 feet, it is the only dry dock in use in the docks today.

In 1872 the Newport Harbour Commissioners decided that an accurate detailed account of the wharves and development along the River Usk, from the river's mouth to the town bridge, should be recorded. It was therefore decided that a photographer should capture the scenes on glass-plate negatives; he chartered a vessel and, mooring at certain points along the river, took a series of photographs, some of which are reproduced here.

Many problems were encountered with the digging out of the North Lock, which were to occur again many years later with the South Dock excavations. On 1 September 1874 the monthly report from Mr Parkinson to the Board of Directors stated that Mr Abernethy would be exceeding the estimate for completion of the docks owing to the exceptional character of the ground upon which the branch railways were being formed, and due to the repeated slips of the embankment, a great portion of which had to be re-formed no fewer than 25 times.

A rare photograph taken in 1872 showing the excavation process taking place at North Dock, with two fixed derricks hard at work. *Newport Harbour Commissioners Office*

Map of the Alexandra Docks, Newport, circa 1884. *Cardiff Public Library*

Another 1872 photograph, showing the newly completed and erected lock gates of the North Lock entrance, with three steam cranes in view. Also on the left-hand side can be seen the new power station buildings that would supply the electric power to this lock. The buildings consisted of a pump and electrical generating house, economiser, water softening and feed pump house. *Newport Harbour Commissioners Office*

The North Dock (Act of 1865)

The North Dock opened for the handling of mineral and general traffic on the same day as the Lock, 10 April 1875. Immediately the opening ceremony was completed, a telegram was dispatched to His Royal Highness the Prince of Wales:

'The Mayor of Newport has the honour most respectfully to inform HRH the Prince of Wales that the Alexandra Dock, named after HRH the Princess of Wales, has been successfully opened in the presence of 40,000 people of all classes and amidst the universal rejoicings of the inhabitants of Wales.'

Within two hours the reply was received:

'The Prince of Wales, Sandringham, to the Mayor of Newport, Mon.

I thank you very much for your telegram, and I congratulate most heartily the inhabitants of Wales on the success of the undertaking.'

During the excavation of the dock the remains of a Viking longship were discovered, lying at a depth of only 12 feet below the surface. Today the depth of water in the dock is 28 feet.

Both the North and South Docks were electrically lit by 1904, this being very much an unprecedented move towards safety; gas was much cheaper but the most dangerous form of lighting in use at the time. Also at that time both docks were equipped with a total of 17 hydraulic coal hoists and 31 cranes of fixed and movable types, all operated by means of hydraulic pressure, created by steam power and ranging in pressure from 1½ tons per square inch to as much as 40 tons per square inch.

After the Grouping of 1922 and the subsequent taking over of the docks by the GWR, improvements were made in all aspects; by 1932 they containing a total of 12 hydraulically operated cranes with a 30-ton lifting capacity, 18 hydraulic cranes with a 6-ton lift, 27 electric cranes also with a 6-ton lift, and nine steam cranes with a lifting capacity of 10 tons.

East Quay (later renamed North Quay)

This quay was the location of the hydraulic cranes Nos 10, 12, 13 and 16 (which were of the movable type, with fixed jib and a lifting capacity of 3 tons), 11, 14 and 15 (movable type with fixed jib but with a lifting capacity of 6 tons), 17 (as 11, 14 and 15 but with a lifting capacity of 30 tons), 18 (fixed type with a fixed jib and a lifting capacity of 2½ tons) and 19 (fixed, with a fixed jib and a lifting capacity of 2 tons). By 1932 the GWR had installed a further eight hydraulic cranes on the East Quay, making a total of 18.

By 1996 this quay was handling scrap metal and some coal imports, and the No 2 warehouse situated on the quay handled cargo trade to the Continent.

Above GWR Macaw B-type bogie bolster No 107027, carrying steel girders and photographed in March 1927 on the 70-ton weighbridge that was located at the East Quay side. On the extreme right can be seen a GWR ventilated van and an ANDR open wagon next to No 1 Transit Shed, North Dock. The extensive railway sidings that once ran along this side of North Dock have now been removed, leaving only a few lines for rail traffic, leading mainly to the No 2 warehouse and the South Docks area. *Associated British Ports*

Left The steamship *Ethelburga* discharges iron ore at the North Dock circa 1900. The photograph also shows some of the 16 hydraulic cranes in use at the time. Three types of lettering are known to have been used on the ANDR open plank wagons, and this view shows that most commonly used. The iron ore trade from these docks ceased in 1975 with the opening of the Port Talbot tidal harbour. *South Glamorgan Libraries*

A washer made to fit the dock's 100-ton crane photographed by the official docks photographer on 14 July 1908, whose task was to record every scene for posterity. *Associated British Ports*

East Quay, North Dock, showing colliery pit-props being stacked and loaded on to Great Western Railway open wagons, en route to the collieries of the Western Valleys, circa 1900. The sailing ships in this photograph are three-masted barques, ideally suited for the carrying of cargoes such as timber or cotton. *ANDR booklet of 1916*

A row of single-plank trucks stands at East Quay circa 1912; the number on the nearest is 32080. The vessel alongside is a type known as a turret ship, that is one built with narrow sides that are superimposed on to a narrow-shaped hull, giving these ships a shape similar to that of a submarine's hull. This is one of a group of ships built to use the Suez Canal on a regular basis, where, because of their shape, they incurred lower toll charges than conventionally built vessels, the charges being based on measurements for tonnage space. This saved their owners a considerable amount of money over a period of time. *ANDR booklet of 1916*

Left This photograph of the storage area for general cargo at East Quay on 4 June 1910 gives a good idea of the varied selection of traffic in use or waiting to be moved from the North Dock. The various wagons and vans consist of mainly tarpaulined four-wheel wagons; the one on the extreme right, numbered 36500, is one of the GWR seven-plank type, while that numbered 43548 looks like a GWR five-plank. A selection of GWR box vans can also be seen, beyond which is what looks like one of the converted ANDR transit vans, and one of the newly acquired Barnum & Bailey coaches. In the background is the Transporter Bridge, Newport's most famous landmark; the row of houses leading towards it is Watch House Parade. *Associated British Ports*

Below left The SS *City of Khios* at berth at East Quay, with railway coaches for the Egyptian State Railways being shipped aboard via 30-ton crane No 17 circa 1910. This vessel was one of the Ellerman Line ships that provided a monthly service from Newport to Aden, Sudan, Mombasa and other East African ports. Built in 1878 by Messrs Barclay Curle & Co, she was equipped with a compound engine of 500 nominal horsepower. *ANDR booklet of 1916*

Top right In about 1917 railway equipment is awaiting shipment to France for use by the War Department during the First World War. The Alexandra Docks handled a tremendous amount of war traffic during the war years, with the Salvage Factory girls working non-stop for the war effort. *Associated British Ports*

Middle right ANDR road vehicle No 4 being loaded with potatoes, helped by volunteers during the General Strike of 1926. Those solid tyres must have provided the driver with a bumpy ride! *Associated British Ports*

Bottom right This 1936 photograph shows the SS *Rushpool* discharging iron ore, her first cargo for Ebbw Vale foundries, into 20-ton iron ore hoppers. This ship, with a gross registered tonnage of 5,125, was built in 1928 but torpedoed by a German submarine while crossing the North Atlantic in January 1941. *Associated British Ports*

Timber Stage, East Side

Located on the east side of North Dock was the Timber Stage, 960 feet long and equipped with nine hydraulic cranes, with a quay wall 1,160 feet long and equipped in 1914 with ten cranes, one of which could deal with loads of up to 30 tons. Also on the east side in 1914 were two large warehouses built for housing general imports.

The cranes situated on the Timber Stage were Nos 1, 2 and 3, with a lifting capacity of 2 tons, and Nos 4 to 8, which were the movable type and had a lifting capacity of 2½ tons. All these cranes had fixed jibs, as did No 9, which had a lifting capacity of 3 tons.

Below The SS *West Harshaw*, a three-island steamer, is seen at the Timber Stage circa 1928 discharging timber over the side into the dock, a risky business at the best of times for those dockers on the floats. *Associated British Ports*

With the amalgamation of the Alexandra Docks into the GWR system in 1922, a considerable amount of money was spent on modernising and improving both North and South Docks. This modernisation included a complete reconstruction of the Timber Stage in re-inforced concrete, additional storage sidings for loaded and empty railway wagons, the adoption of coaling appliances for the emptying of 20-ton coal wagons, and the replacement of hydraulically operated cranes with the newer electrically operated luffing cranes. By 1934 the GWR had also provided additional sidings next to the Timber Stage for the handling and storage of general cargo traffic.

Top right This 26 January 1927 view, again of the Timber Stage, gives quite a clear picture of the cranes purchased from Messrs Armstrong Whitworth Company in 1906. Also in view is engine No 676, originally Alexandra Docks No 3;

it was withdrawn by the GWR in 1929, scarcely two years after this picture was taken. *Associated British Ports*

Middle right This busy scene was taken from near the ANDR Dock Company offices in September 1926, looking northwards in the direction of Watch House Parade. On the left are the cranes at the former East Quay, by then known as North Quay, with various open-type wagons in view belonging to the London, Midland & Scottish Railway and the pre-Grouping Great Eastern, Great Western and North Eastern companies. The steel hoppers are from the Blaenavon Big Pit Colliery. In front of the camera are GWR bolster wagons with loads of telegraph poles awaiting transportation, while on the right are GWR open six-plank wagons. Two have tarpaulin sheet rails fitted, while the remainder may be part of a common user wagon pool rather than being restricted to the GWR system. It looks as though some of them have transported animal feeds to the docks, judging by the amount of hay left in them. *Associated British Ports*

Bottom right This photograph was taken a little further north, also about 1926 and also facing towards Newport town. On the extreme left can be seen the Timber Stage at the north end of North Dock (with the inevitable timber stacked up to over 30 feet high), and the road leading towards the dock gates, with what appears to be one of the dock's 1½-ton road vehicles. The sidings in front of the camera are quite congested with LMS and GWR open wagons loaded with sorted planks of various thickness, the bolster wagons carrying the heavier planks. On the right there seem to be a lot of internal-user-only wagons. Also on the right are empty GWR bolster bogie wagons, and next to them Private Owner colliery wagons from the United National Collieries, and a group from the Black Vein Collieries, Risca. On the extreme right are the coaling hoists of the ANDR-built River Wharf. The large building in the right background is the Mersey Insulation Company's works. In the far distance one of the ANDR shunting engines is about to pick up some of the empty wagons. All in all, a very busy scene indeed! *Associated British Ports*

ANDR engine No 19, an 0-6-0 saddle tank, at work around the North Dock on 31 July 1905, hence the use of spare chains and oil cans. One of the ANDR two-plank open wagons can also be seen, possibly on shunting duties. No 19 was built by Messrs Peckett in 1886, renumbered by the GWR as 680, and eventually scrapped in 1948. *LCGB (Ken Nunn Collection)*

West Side

The coaling hoists of the North Dock were located on the west side, and by 1914 consisted of three movable hoists. These were numbered by the ANDR as Nos 1, 2 and 7; Nos 1 and 2 had a lift of 48 feet above coping level, and No 7 a lift of 28ft 9in. In addition to these movable hoists there were six hoists of the fixed type, numbered 3, 4, 5 and 6; Nos 3 and 5 had a lift above coping level of 46 feet, Nos 4 and 6 only 28ft 6in. The other two hoists on this side were lettered A and B and were situated on projecting jetties, having a lift of 27ft 9in. These coaling hoists were operated hydraulically and had three lines of rails leading to them from the Marshalling Sidings situated further over to the west.

In the *GWR Magazine* of 1932 a short article appeared with reference to the North Docks:

'Newport. A new movable hoist having a lifting capacity above water level of 66 feet, with low and high level traversers for loaded and empty wagons, respectively, and capable of dealing with 20 ton wagons, had been erected in substitution of number 6 hoist, North dock, thus the company completes a pledge given to the people of Newport, that when the powers were obtained by the Company's Act of 1929 to close the Old Town Dock, the company then agreed with the corporation to remove two hoists from the Town Dock to the Alexandra Dock, and erect a movable hoist at the latter dock.'

The article also stated that five new 3-ton electric cranes had been provided on the South Quay side of the South Docks.

All the coal hoists and the extensive sidings had been finally removed by the 1960s, and by 1996 only the jetties of A and B remained; too costly to remove, they served as a reminder of busier times. This area was then the main stacking area for the storage of timber, under the guidance and supervision of Messrs Meyer South & West Limited.

Above By 1906 the coal and fuel exports handled from the Alexandra Docks amounted to 5,104,990 tons, an increase of 973,320 tons since 1896 (4,131,670 tons), and was to rise to over 6 million tons by 1914. This photograph shows the loading of coal aboard a vessel in North Dock circa 1900. In the background can be seen the tall masts of wooden sailing ships, still a common sight even at this late period of shipping technology. *South Glamorgan Libraries*

Below left Movable hoists on the west side of North Dock, circa 1900; the one nearest the camera is No 2. *Associated British Ports*

Below One of the fixed hoists, in this case No 5, circa 1917. Beyond can be seen the viaducts, or 'roads' as they were known, from Nos 6, 7 and 8 hoists, which led the empty wagons back to the storage sidings. *Associated British Ports*

Above Open-type colliery wagons from the Tir Pentwys Black Vein Colliery Company, in this case carrying coal from the Tir Pentwys Colliery at Pontypool, at the No 5 hoist at North Dock circa 1904. Syren and Shipping *magazine*

Left A Partridge, Jones & Company advertisement from the ANDR booklet of 1914. *Associated British Ports*

Below Colliery wagons of Partridge, Jones & Company of Abersychen, circa 1900, in this case belonging to the Blaensychen Colliery. *South Glamorgan Libraries*

Partridge, Jones & Co.,
Limited,
Colliery Proprietors,   NEWPORT Mon.

PROPRIETORS AND SHIPPERS OF THE CELEBRATED

**Western Valley Black Vein Steam Coal.
Mynydd Black Vein Steam Coal.
Locomotive, House, Gas, and Manufacturing Coals**

Shipping Ports: Newport, Cardiff and Barry

Telegrams: Telephones
"Partridge, Newport-Mon"   Post Office, No. 21; National, No. 304

Right Colliery wagons of the Powell Duffryn Steam Coal Company of New Tredegar, belonging to the East & West Elliot Pits, New Tredegar, circa 1900. *South Glamorgan Libraries*

Below Coal awaiting shipment, in wagons belonging to the Albion Black Vein Colliery and the John Blundell Black Vein Colliery of Pontypool (left), and in six-plank open wagons of Bailey & Roberts (right), circa 1900. *South Glamorgan Libraries*

Left Private Owner wagons of the United National Colliery Company carrying coal from the Black Vein Colliery, Risca, circa 1900. *South Glamorgan Libraries*

The firm of Burt Bolton & Hayward is also located at the west side of the docks. This long-established business deals with the storage and handling, as well as the creosote treatment, of all forms of timber from telegraph poles to planed planks. It occupies the site of the former Messrs Batchelors works, a family firm that was established in 1812. This photograph shows wood being off-loaded at the west side of North Dock circa 1900, most of it being pitwood from Scandinavia and North America, en route to the collieries of the Rhondda and Western Valleys. *South Glamorgan Libraries*

Timber Float, West Side

The Timber Float, located on the west side of the North Dock, was opened in 1878; it ran parallel with the North Dock, and covered an area of some 10 acres, with a depth of 8 feet, being connected to the North Dock via a canal. All logs floated through this canal were counted and numbered individually. It is interesting that, when completed, the dock was filled with fresh water, not sea water, mainly at the wishes of the traders of Newport, who were to use the facilities of these docks.

Later, possibly by 1916, the GWR added another Timber Float, also running parallel and situated a short distance from the original ANDR float; this one covered an area of 5¼ acres.

By 1996 the canal and timber floats had long been filled in and this area was also a part of the extensive timber storage yard used by Messrs Meyer East & West Limited.

The River Wharf

The River Wharf was located on the west bank of the River Usk, adjoining the entrance to the Alexandra North Dock. It had quayage of 403 feet, and was equipped with four movable cranes. Nos 28, 29 and 30 were installed in 1906, and No 31 in 1919; they were renumbered as 58, 59, 60 and 61 in 1930. They all had fixed jibs and a lifting capacity of 2 tons.

Plans for the building of this wharf were drawn up by the end of 1904, with the work starting in 1905. It was renamed by the GWR as the GWR Wharf and closed just prior to the start of the Second World War, but was re-opened for the handling and shipping of coal to the Bristol and Avonmouth Docks. It even handled to a limited degree some coal exports to the Continent.

Right River Wharf, sometimes called Riverside Wharf, under construction in November 1905. This photograph gives a good idea on the use of the steel pile-drivers; as can be seen this one is poised ready to be driven downwards. This action was repeated time and time again until a sufficiently deep hole was made to take the main supports of the jetty. In the background can be seen the Transporter Bridge, also under construction, with scaffolding in evidence at the top of the western tower. *Associated British Ports*

Right Another view of River Wharf under construction in October 1905. *Associated British Ports*

Below River Wharf with the navvies, gangers and contractors, including dog, posing upon what appears to be the finished job, circa 1906. The Transporter Bridge was also opened on 12 September of that year. *Associated British Ports*

British Transport Commission map of the Alexandra Docks, circa 1960. In the top right-hand corner is Park Junction, and the PC&N connection from there to West Mendalgief Junction, just across the South Wales main line, is shown as lifted. At the junction of the sidings complex and the entrance to North Dock is Mendalgief East Junction. Maesglas Junction is north of West Mendalgief, above Alexandra Dock Junction on the South Wales main line. *Associated British Ports*

This excellent photograph gives a good indication of the layout of and activity within the docks circa 1922. In the foreground are the various jetties of the River Wharf area jutting out into the River Usk, some of the privately owned ones by now in a state of neglect, possibly as a result of the decline of the coal trade. Beyond the jetties on the extreme left-hand side of the photograph can be seen the North Lock and the entrance into North Dock; although it still contains water, the lock was out of use by this time. A short distance to the right can be seen No 2 shed, then over on the west side the vast area of sidings and coal hoists, behind which can just be seen the Timber Float. Stretching away into the distance is the River Ebbw, and joining North Dock to South Dock is Junction Cut with its swingbridge in the closed position. Beyond is South Dock, with the coal hoists on its west side marking its boundary. *Courtesy John Cornwall*

Alexandra Graving Dock
(entered from the North Dock)

This Graving Dock was situated at the south-east corner of the North Dock, and measured 532 feet from the gates to the head of the dock, the width of the entrance being 50 feet, and the dock width 74 feet. Today no trace is left of it, as it has been completely filled in.

Dry docks

Alexandra Docks contained a Commercial Dry Dock with an entrance from the North Dock. It was 523 feet long and 74 feet wide; the entrance measured 49ft 11in wide, which became 50 feet with the removal of the batter (inward inclination) on the entrance walls in 1934, the depth of water remaining at 20 feet to the outer sills. The ship repairs in this dock were carried out by whoever the ship-owner selected. The Commercial Dry Dock was filled in by 1958.

In addition, there were six private dry docks located nearby, with entrances from the River Usk; the largest, that of the Cardiff Channel Dry Dock & Pontoon Company Limited, was 785 feet long, with an entrance 65 feet wide. Others were the Eastern Dry Dock, measuring 360 feet long by 57 feet wide, later lengthened to 430 feet, and by 1934 under the ownership of the Mountstuart Dry Dock Company; the Mary Dry Dock, 350 feet long by 60 feet wide; the Alice Dry Dock, 289 feet by 46ft 6in; and the Edith Dry Dock, 220 feet by 36 feet. These four dry docks were owned by Messrs Mordey, Carney & Company Ltd. Finally there was the Tredegar Dry Dock, owned by the Tredegar Dry Dock & Wharf Company Ltd, which was 712 feet long with a width of 65 feet. By 1934 this dock had also passed into the ownership of Mountstuart.

North Dock Central Hydraulic Power Station

The Central Power Station provided the power to operate almost all of the facilities in the docks, including hoists, hydraulic cranes, lock gates, the Rolling Bridge, swingbridge, capstans, etc, and was situated at the north end of North Dock. It was of brick construction, consisting of the engine house, boiler house, pump house and economiser house. At the south end of this building stood the chimney stack, which rose to a height of 140 feet, and near the chimney were three storage and controlling accumulators.

Steam was supplied to the engines, of which there were four, at a pressure of 185lb per square inch, generated in a range of seven Lancaster boilers, to give a blow-off pressure of 200lb. The temperature of the water, obtained from the town's supply and also from the ANDR company's own fresh water supply, was raised from 40 degrees to 400 degrees Fahrenheit.

Subsequently this power station was converted into engineering shops, and today all traces of it have long gone.

The three-masted vessel *Celestial Empire* in the Commercial Dry Dock. Records show that this vessel was in dry dock from 31 July to 2 August 1906, docked stern first, with the barque *Edward Preeg*. *Associated British Ports*

The North Dock today

Today's Alexandra Docks, under the ownership and guidance of Associated British Ports, have changed almost beyond belief from the original design and concept of Lord Tredegar, but one cannot help but feel that they have lived up to and perhaps surpassed the expectations of the ANDR General Manager, John Macauley, who was very much a man of vision. Although today the coal trade is not handled to the scale that it once was, there have been other developments that have replaced it.

Today on the east side of the North Dock is the firm of W. E. Dowds, Shipping, Limited, offering a dedicated gantry-served import facility, with a weighbridge and large waiting area for road traffic; the storage sheds numbered 2, 2A and 2B, holding imported steel, are located here. Next to W. E. Dowds is Island Steel, which provides a convenient steel-slitting facility to the port's customers, as well as a 24-hour weighbridge service. This quay is also used for the berthing of tugs, including the Cory tug *Bargarth*, when not in use.

At present moored at the former Timber Stage in the north-east corner, and a short distance from the top of this dock, is the preserved passenger ferry *Southsea*, of Portsmouth, undergoing repairs and restoration by members of the Avon River Historical Vessel & Navigational Trust Group.

The north side of the North Dock is now quite overgrown with water-weeds and bulrushes providing a haven for the water-birds that inhabit this dock, especially for the pair of mute swans – a secluded yet peaceful scene that contrasts strongly with the bustle of activity around this industrial setting. Situated alongside the North Dock road at the north-west corner of the dock is the creosote works of the long-established firm of Messrs Burt Bolton & Hayward. Almost all of the timber, which comes from Scandinavia and the Baltic regions, in the form of telegraph poles, awaiting timber treatment or a creosote bath. The company is now part of the Finnforest Timber Company Group, a combination that should do well.

A short distance from Burt Bolton's yard is a large area occupied by the building and general trade supplier Jewson, incorporating not only the company's roofed premises but also a timber storage yard with storage sheds for imported stocks of East Russian and South American timber. At the rear of these timber sheds can be seen the remains of the trackbed that carried the line along the west side of this dock from West Mendalgief Junction down to the former coaling hoists at South Dock; this once busy place is now inhabited by Buddleia bushes, providing a show of lilac and yellow, with birds and butterflies in abundance, as well as patches of grass and weeds surviving well between the ballast and sleepers. Located in a corner of the Jewson complex is the Snowflake firm, a Newport-based supplier of bagged sawdust and wood shavings for animal bedding use throughout England and Wales.

Almost alongside Junction Cut on this west side is the dredging firm of Severn Sands, dealing in sand and aggregates and making regular trips to various parts of the Bristol Channel with its own vessel, the aptly named *Severn Sands*. Once the cargo is graded, washed and bagged, delivery is made by road transport from these docks to building suppliers such as Travis Perkins. Not far from the Severn Sands premises is the mooring point for the docks tug *Emsgarth*.

Also in the Junction Cut area, on the east side, is C. H. Bailey's Dry Dock, which is still going strong, and for many years has been the only dry dock here. The ANDR booklet of 1914 states that C. H. Bailey was the first company to utilise hydraulic jacks for raising collapsed furnace crowns, and also described the use of special machinery for the making of shafts; the 30-ton shaft lathes could take off five cuts at the same time as the coupling holes were bored. With such early skills it is little wonder that this firm still exists. During a visit in July 2001 I watched the docks tug *El Preston* undergoing an overhaul inside the dock, while moored outside was the passenger ferry *Welsh Liberty*, owned by Bailey's and currently undergoing refurbishment by the firm. Such expertise deserves rewards, and I am sure that this company will be here for many more years. The entrance arms, which guided vessels into this former lock from the River Usk, are still visible.

In the same area, in front of the two Riverside Cottages, is the ANDR headquarters building, and between it and the cottages is now the main running line into the docks, leading south-east past the North Dock staging area and North Quay towards Middle Quay, South Dock, after which it turns westwards to end at the quayside of South Quay, South Dock.

The concrete Riverside Wharf, on the River Usk near Riverside Cottages, is long gone, and only the dilapidated remains of the jetty are still visible today, its weathered planks and timber held together with rusty nuts and bolts.

The red-brick ANDR headquarters building is still in use as the main office for the docks, a role that has never really changed over the years. It may not be as impressive a building as the Gothic-styled Pierhead building at Cardiff Docks, but it is a solidly built structure. As one enters the foyer two ships' bells catch the eye, one from the *Newport* and the other from the *Uskmouth*, while on the walls and stairway are old photographs, some of which are featured in this book. Entering the impressive boardroom one cannot help but feel a sense of reverence. On one side is the large, japanned, decorative cast iron fireplace, while more photographs decorate the walls, but the most striking feature of the room is the massive boardroom table. It was on this table that I carefully placed the ANDR photograph albums and saw for the first time what you see today in this book. By contrast, when I photographed the

Cardiff Docks archives many years ago, I stood beside a fireproof safe-like door inside a large dark vault, lit only by two single fluorescent lights, one in each aisle, not at all like the spacious ANDR boardroom with its large windows.

Next to this building, and contrasted to its very red brickwork, is the engineering department, of decorative, light brown brick, strengthened with light grey stone edging.

In the south-east corner of North Dock, near the Junction Cut opening, are the still visible remains of the former Commercial Dry Dock; although long ago filled in, its shape can still be plainly seen, overgrown with weeds, grass, and an abundance of ox-eye daisies. It is at the entrance to this dock, located a short distance from C. H. Bailey's premises, that the vessel *Welsh Liberty* is moored.

On the other side of the cobbled road from the Commercial Dry Dock are the Central Workshops. Today these former GWR engineering works are in a very neglected state, and are due for demolition soon. Built in blue pennant stone, with cream-coloured brickwork lining the windows and doors, it is a building to equal any Station Master's house! At present the premises are used by the port supplies department, but for how much longer is anybody's guess.

North Dock, photographed from the west side looking towards the former Timber Stage on 27 July 2001. The vessel *Southsea*, of Portsmouth, is awaiting its forthcoming restoration. The reeds at the top of the dock, on the left, add a splash of green to the waters, while nearer the camera numerous seabirds rest on the remains of a coaling jetty. *Author*

2. THE SOUTH DOCK

Junction Cut (Swingbridge Junction)

Junction Cut is situated between the North and South Docks, connecting them via a channel about 60 feet in width. It was spanned by a swingbridge 125 feet long, which connected the west side of North Dock with the east side of South Dock; the bridge was operated hydraulically, the machinery being supplied by Sir W. G. Armstrong Mitchell & Company Ltd. It was over this swingbridge that rail access was gained to the original engine shed of 1875.

Today this cut is little more than a channel between two docks, a little overgrown in places, with the land on either side providing plenty of cover for the nests of water-birds.

Junction Cut, or Swingbridge Junction as it was also known, in about 1934 – Alexandra Dock divers are about to commence work on the deepening of the lock by the removal of the lock inverts. This photograph is also quite historic, as it records for the first time the use of pneumatic drills underwater. This was to be a trial run of great importance.

Left to right: linesman F. Kilby (later to become a diver himself); diver Joe Wallis (father of Arthur Wallis); Inspector Bert Gumbrill; unknown (a representative of the firm making the drills); diver Fred Lewis; and linesman Arthur Lewis. *Courtesy of the late Mr A. Wallis*

The South Lock (Act of 1882)

This was the original entrance to the South Dock; opened in 1893, it enabled vessels to reach the South Dock from the River Usk. It was built to a length of 503ft 6in and a width of 72 feet, and maintained a water depth in the lock of 25 feet, rising to 35 feet during spring tides.

South Lock was renamed East Lock with the opening of the new South Lock in 1914, and was closed during the middle period of the First World War, possibly 1916, although it was still regarded as an emergency entrance to the docks for many years until finally being partially filled in during 1937.

Access for road and rail traffic to the South Quay of South Dock across the original South Lock was gained by crossing a roller bridge, built in 1909. Originally this bridge carried a double set of railway lines, set in the ground as was usual in industrial locations, and was also provided with an overhung footbridge for pedestrian use.

The travel of this bridge was 107 feet, and the whole structure was carried on brick piers with cast iron cylinders. Railway signals, guarding the approaches to the bridge, were located on either side of the gates. The levers to operate the bridge were located in a signal cabin on the north side of the lock.

After the lines to the Salvage Factory were extended the bridge was fixed in position, the name changing to Rolling Bridge Junction in 1915.

The rolling bridge on 12 December 1908, during its construction. It was provided to carry road and rail traffic over the original South Lock for access to the South Dock Extension work. The signal box erected at Roller Bridge Crossing was there not only for the movement of railway traffic but also as an observation post to offset the likelihood of any accidents when the bridge was in the open position. *Associated British Ports*

Left An ANDR map of April 1914 showing the North and South Docks and the South Dock Extension. *Courtesy Mr D. C. Sims*

Above An aerial view corresponding to the map opposite (the dark patches are the shadows of clouds). Taken in 1948, it gives a good view of the Timber Float on the right, while in the middle left can be seen the arms of the original North Lock entrance. Below that the riverside River Wharf coal hoists are still standing, although some of the runs leading to the coal hoists on the west side of North Dock have been taken up. Junction Cut can also be clearly seen joining the North and South Docks. In the top right-hand corner is South Lock. The blocks of houses in the bottom left-hand corner consist of Watch House Parade, Alexandra Road and Mendalgief Road, and to the right of them is the ANDR's Pill engine shed. *Associated British Ports*

The new South Lock
(Act of 1906)

The new South Lock was also known as the Great Sea Lock, as the entrance was from the Bristol Channel and not the River Usk as in the older lock. Work was started by the contractors, Messrs Easton Gibb & Son, in December 1906, and the work took many years, the new lock not being completed until 1914. On 14 July of that year it was officially opened by HRH Prince Arthur of Connaught, son of HM King George V.

The lock has a total length of 1,000 feet and a width of 100 feet, being divided by watertight gates into two compartments of 600 and 400 feet respectively. Today it is the only entrance into the docks.

Notes in the Associated British Ports archive state that the first vessel into the South Dock via the newly opened South Lock was the steam yacht *Liberty*, built in 1908 and owned by Lord Tredegar; it broke a ribbon that had been placed across the lock entrance, and was then secured alongside the pump house.

After declaring the lock open, Prince Arthur and the dignitaries disembarked to inspect the pump house and staff before re-embarking to continue their passage into the South Dock.

ADR

Luncheon

on the occasion of the opening of

The New Entrance Lock

of the

Alexandra (Newport & South Wales)

Docks & Railway

by

H.R.H. Prince Arthur of Connaught, K.G.

on Tuesday, 14th July, 1914.

Above The luncheon invitation on the opening of the new South Lock, 14 July 1914. *Courtesy Newport Public Library*

Below The new South Lock under construction on 21 May 1908, with contractors' temporary lines and shoring timber much in evidence. Also in view is the river bed of the diverted River Ebbw. *Associated British Ports*

Above The view looking eastwards from the inner end of the new South Lock on 20 June 1908. The eastern section of the lock was opened in 1907. *Associated British Ports*

Below A close-up of the Manning Wardle contractor's engine seen in the previous photograph. On the right can be seen one of the contractor's steam cranes, with plenty of temporary track; although sharply curved and uneven, the heavy loads that this type of track withstood during this excavation work on these docks was quite remarkable. *Associated British Ports*

Above This photograph, dated 27 July 1908, was taken by the official Alexandra Dock photographer, employed to record the building and excavation of the South Lock and Dock. It shows two of the contractors posing next to one of the steel piles used for drilling the jetty foundations for the new South Lock entrance. These piles would be driven down under great pressure, hence the pointed end, specially made for this essential work. *Associated British Ports*

Below Contractors on the site of the new entrance jetties, 24 October 1908. The problems overcome by the type of soil encountered were numerous; described by them as liquid mud, it can quite easily be seen here clinging to the men, the dredging bucket and just about everything else in sight! *Associated British Ports*

The excavated site of the Middle Gates area of the new South Lock on 19 November 1909. Note the inevitable steam cranes and what appear to be metal-studded, possibly reinforced, contractors' wagons, all fitted with 'dumb buffers', ie wooden blocks. These wagons were made by the contractors themselves to carry the tremendous weight of the heavy soil. In the background can be seen one of the temporary water tanks, and to its right the rotary cement mixer. *Associated British Ports*

The South Dock (Act of 1882) and South Dock Extension (Act of 1904)

The original length of the South Dock when opened on 6 June 1893 was 1,500 feet, with a width of 650 feet, thus covering an area of some 20 acres. The tonnage of vessels using the North Dock increased dramatically by no less than three-quarters of a million tons even while the new dock was being constructed. One advantage of the new South Dock was that the larger vessels entering the North Dock could now do so via the newly opened South Lock (later the East Lock), as the depth of water in this lock was the same as that of the North Dock.

However, after a while it was obvious that yet further expansion would be needed to handle the ever-increasing traffic, and by 1903 plans were put into operation to extend once again. The surveying work started in 1904, carried out by Mr Cuthbert and Mr Brereton MInstCE for the firm of Sir John Woolfe Barry & Partners, the resident ANDR engineer being Mr J. D. C. Couper.

The excavation work for the first part of the South Dock Extension was again contracted to Messrs Easton Gibb & Son of Westminster in May 1905, and they wasted no time. Work started in the June of that year to recover the 48 acres required.

In September 1907 the ANDR recorded: 'Situated between the South Dock (in the bank) and the first part of this extension (which was the former entrances to the timber float) piles were driven to secure the junction of this extension, with a formal agreement taking place that this would be the spot at which to make the sluice gate required to fill this extension with water from the existing dock, which would find its own way down into the newly excavated area of 48 acres. To effect this a portion of the piles were cut away to a depth of 10 feet and a large sluice gate was placed

The newly started excavation work on the new South Dock Extension in about 1904; it can be seen how the shape is being formed as layer after layer of soil is removed. Also in view is one of the contractor's engines with what looks like a full load. *Associated British Ports*

One of the contractor's steam navvies is seen here at work circa 1908 beside one of the former farm buildings that was situated on the land before it was acquired for the dock extension. *Associated British Ports*

in that space, temporary piles having already been driven in.

'When the time was right, at a given moment these piles were lifted up by one of the travelling cranes; with the clay of the embankment having already been cut away and the stones removed, the way was clear. Steadily a trickle of water began its journey down this man-made chute, finding its own way to its destination. When the cutting of this bank had proceeded far enough, the sluice gate was again raised and the stream of water again began its flow into the newly extended dock. A total of between 400,000,000 and 450,000,000 gallons of water was required. This work took nearly a month

before the correct levels were obtained, with the remainder of the water being pumped into one of the cut-off parts of the River Ebbw.'

The bank referred to was dredged and the sludge pumped into another part of the disused area of the River Ebbw.

The ANDR booklet of 1914 stated that one of the most difficult undertakings of the extension work was the damming of the River Ebbw, which had to be undertaken at four different points at each end of the diversion, the aim being to close the old channel, and at the north and south sides of the dock respectively, to complete the quay that enclosed the extension.

Many thousands of tons of wood were needed for shoring up the excavations during the construction of the South Dock Extension. This photograph gives an idea of how stout the timbers had to be to be able to withstand the tremendous pressure that was applied to the cross-bracings of the excavation trenches. Photographed on 24 August 1908. *Associated British Ports*

A very clear description of the work undertaken by Easton Gibb & Son was outlined in the ANDR company booklet of 1906:

'Speaking generally, the level of the ground on the dock site was 6 to 7 feet lower than the level of the quay, and as the area was desired for siding accommodation it has all to be embanked to the latter level. A large proportion of the excavation has had to be taken out in the dry, for the formation of these extensive embankments means that the material has to be taken partly from that area of the extension lying to the east of the River Ebbw, and partly from the site of the river diversion.

'On the former site, the method used differed. The total depth of 39 feet has been tackled in three lifts of about 13 feet each with an occasional four lifts where the original ground level was somewhat higher. The excavated material is drawn from the bottom of the dock, up two inclines, one on the south and one of the north side of the extension, and this is then led to the spoil banks. No winding engines have been employed as the locomotive power is amply sufficient for the gradients in use.

'While making its first cut in any lift, the steam navvy is driven forward and downward, working in a "gullet", that is cutting on both sides. When the desired depth of lift has been obtained, the machine moves forward on the level, but still cutting on both sides. Upon the first cut being completed the steam navvy is drawn back, and again moves forward, cutting only one side and thus widening the gullet, and so on, until the first lift is complete over the required area.

'A somewhat different method was used for the removal of the quantity of material in the River Ebbw diversion, which it was necessary to excavate in the dry. Here the shape of the cutting and its great length, as compared with its width, and the extreme flatness of the slopes, went against the use of what may be called the "incline and gullet" system.

Above It was on the east side near this location that the first engine shed, built in 1875, was situated. By 1890 this two-road shed, quoted as being 123ft 6in long by 33 feet wide, was insufficient to house and cope with the increased locomotive work needed by the contractors working on the South Dock Extension, so in 1904 the contractors built their own shed to house their Manning Wardle engines. The newly built shed, made of corrugated tin sheeting and with a temporary water tank nearby, is seen here. *Associated British Ports*

Left This slightly different view of the same location shows one of the contractor's Manning Wardle engines circa 1904. A total of five were used by Messrs Easton Gibb & Son during the excavation work. *Associated British Ports*

Accordingly a bucket land dredger of the "Lubecker" type was brought into use. This machine, by the manipulation of its ladder, is able to cut the slope to any required angle, or incline, and has the further advantage of excavating to a considerable depth, below the level of the rails on which it stands, thus avoiding the necessity of using gradients as in the case of the steam navvies.

'For the conveyance of excavated material from the cutting, the Lubecker machine is self-propelling, and while working passes slowly over a stationary train of wagons, delivering into these the contents of its bucket. The ladder carrying the buckets works over the side instead of fore and aft, as in a floating dredger. The top lift of the diversion to a depth of 14 feet has been completed by this machine in a series of parallel cuts, the flood bank at either end being left intact to prevent the ingress of water. The quantity still to be removed from the diversion will be taken out by sea dredger, which has already made considerable progress with this work.

'The part of the extension laying between the west bank of the River Ebbw and the site of the diversion has been taken out to the full depth by means of dredging, the river being tidal with a range of 34 feet at spring tides and 15 feet at neap tides. The dredging was necessarily intermittent, with no work being possible at low water.'

Many problems were faced during these excavations. Because of the tidal flow of the River Ebbw, work had to be done by day and night; this cut a normal four-year contract down to around two years, but because artificial lighting was used the normal risks involved with excavation and shunting were increased threefold. Other difficulties were also met and overcome – even the soil was treacherous, as it was of an alluvial deposit known as 'bungham', which needed only the briefest spell of rain to convert it into a liquid mud. Eventually upwards of 3,600,000 tons of this deposit was excavated.

This bungham deposit also had a very adhesive quality, which caused the service roads to sink, even though as many as three or four layers of close timbers had been sunk to provide a suitable foundation. Even the angle of the banks could only be achieved at an angle of not more than four to one, and that 'with difficulty'.

The dry excavation work was undertaken by Messrs Ruston, Proctor & Company, with the use of their steam navvy of the Lubecker bucket type, already referred to. A costly but powerful machine, of which it was the only example in the country, it saved many, many hours of manual labour.

The removal of the excavated material to the spoil banks was accomplished by the use of a small army of locomotives owned by Messrs Manning Wardle & Company, as well as the use of several hundred side-tip wagons, specially built by the contractors themselves and of a size larger than previously used in public works. For the excavation in the 'wet' a large

sea dredger, three powerful tugs and a number of dumb hopper barges of 500-ton capacity worked day and night, a tremendous achievement.

With the 48 acres added, this Extension was opened in November 1907; finally a further 27 acres was added, which was opened, along with the South Lock, on 14 July 1914. This brought the total area covered by land to 110 acres and a total water surface of 96 acres, with a depth of 33 feet; later this was dredged to 38 feet. During 1906 two coal hoists were built for the Extension, each being capable of handling loaded coal wagons with a gross weight of 23 tons. These were supplemented by another two hoists in 1908.

After the Grouping of the railways and docks during the 1922 to 1923 period, the Alexandra (Newport & South Wales) Docks & Railway Company became known as the Great Western Railway's Newport Docks. By 1934 they had a total of 27 electrically operated cranes, and 12 that were hydraulically operated, with the length of the completed South Dock being 4,000 feet, and 1,000 feet wide.

In 1908 the siding accommodation on the north side of South Dock, including goods sheds, covered an area of 600,000 square yards, with a total amount of track within the Alexandra Docks complex of over 100 miles. By 1932 the South Dock had seven transit sheds, which covered a floor area of 708,855 square feet. These sheds contained the various commodities, including grain, flour, general merchandise and even building sand, to name but a few, that were handled by the docks before the Second World War.

This photograph, taken on 1 September 1910 and looking northwards towards the inner gates on the east side, shows in the background the finished 12-foot diameter delivery culvert in place in the east side of the South Lock walls. This culvert will carry water from the River Usk through into the new South Dock, impounding 10 million gallons of water per hour. *Associated British Ports*

South Quay

Built by Messrs Easton Gibb & Son during the extension work of the South Dock, the South Quay consisted of a concrete wall some 3,600 feet long, which by 1914 was equipped with 20 hydraulic cranes having a varied lifting capacity of between 1½ and 10 tons. The length of the quay was sufficient in length to berth nine vessels of an average of 400 feet in length. Also by 1914 siding accommodation had been laid, with a large warehouse 500 feet long by 100 feet wide, equipped for the handling of all types of miscellaneous goods.

The hydraulic cranes located on the South Quay were numbered 32, 34, 35 and 36; they were of the movable type, with luffing jibs and a lifting capacity of 3 tons 3 cwt; similar to these were numbers 44 to 51, also of the movable type with luffing jibs, but capable of lifting weights of 6, 4 and 2 tons. The remaining cranes, numbers 33, 37 and 42, were also of the movable type with lifting capacities of 6, 4 and 2 tons and luffing jibs, and

finally there was one crane with a lifting capacity of 10, 6½ and 3¼ tons.

In 1934 a petrol-driven mobile crane was purchased by the GWR for use in the sheds on this quay. In the same year five electric capstans and 29 reels were installed to assist with the haulage of the railway wagons and the movable cranes.

Apart from the First World War workmen's service from the dock gates to the factory, the ANDR proposed a service from the dock gates to South Quay. The company wrote to the Board of Trade on 13 March 1919: 'Proposed to inaugurate a service of trains for general cargo workers between the entrance and South Quay. One train each way at 7.45am and returning at 5.10pm or thereabouts. Already a platform for service now run to Factory for Ministry of Munitions.' The outcome is unclear, but the proposed service would have used the same route from the entrance as far as Rolling Bridge Junction, from where it would have used the tracks direct to South Quay.

Left South Dock from the air in about 1935 – this photograph, taken from the southern point of the completed South Dock facing south-east, shows on the left the coaling hoists on the North Quay, with hoist No 19 nearest the camera and No 14 furthest away. At the top left-hand corner is the East Lock and No 4 Transit Shed at the East Quay. On the right are vessels at berth at South Quay. The foremost vessel is berthed next to the No 7 Transit Shed, with No 6 Transit Shed in the middle of the quay. The River Usk can be seen in the distance. The three ships moored together at the bottom of this photograph are situated next to No 20 coal hoist. *Associated British Ports*

Top right Oil tank wagons destined for Brazil being loaded aboard at South Quay in October 1929. These eight-wheeled wagons are probably of 20 tons tare, and would have had a wheel gauge of 3ft 3⅜in, or 5ft 3in if they were destined for Central Brazil. Made by the Gloucester Wagon Company, they are from a consignment ordered by the Anglo Mexican Petroleum Company, whose emblem, an ancient Inca Indian sign for good fortune, is seen on the tank sides. *Associated British Ports*

Middle right Manning Wardle engine *Assam* being loaded aboard at South Quay in September 1925. Fitted with the Ramsbottom safety valves and of an 1880s design, it is being shipped to the Rio Branco in South America to become Rio Grande engine No 105. *Associated British Ports*

Bottom right Discharging coils of steel wire and steel bars direct into the waiting wagons via the new electric cranes from Messrs Stothert & Pitt of Bath, seen here next to one of the Transit Sheds at South Quay in March 1927. *Associated British Ports*

Above SS *Elmsport* berthed at South Quay in May 1928, with No 5 Transit Shed in the background on the extreme right. As can be seen, general goods, in this case sacks of grain and pipes, are being transferred aboard ship, the latter from GWR 'Macaw' bogie bolster wagons. The wagon on the left is a GWR five-plank open, numbered 81757; the end-swivel tarpaulin rail can be clearly seen. This rail was officially known as the Williams Patent Sheet Rail, and allowed a tarpaulin sheet to be placed above open wagon loads, thus protecting certain types of goods that might be damaged by rain. The GWR 12 tons tare five-plank open wagon was the mainstay of the GWR fleet for many years, and with this tarpaulin rail fitted it was a very useful merchandise wagon from its introduction in 1901 until the mid-1960s. The box van is of LMS design. *Associated British Ports*

Below SS *City of Christiania*, built in 1921 and of 4,900 GRT, is seen having 1,800 tons of steel sleepers loaded aboard, while berthed at No 2 section of South Quay, near No 6 transit shed, on 11 May 1928. The steel sleepers are probably en route to a country that has a termite problem, possibly Africa. *Associated British Ports*

Above A cargo of Russian timber being discharged from the Russian vessel *Dvinoles* at berth in South Dock circa 1930. The vessel behind is the SS *Sunmoss*. The Stothert & Pitt cranes are unloading into former GWR five-plank open wagons, some of which are for internal dock use only. Wagon number 067264 in the centre carries the inscription 'For use of sand', and 'Grabs only'. *Associated British Ports*

Below Another view showing Stothert & Pitt cranes at South Quay, this time loading general cargo in March 1955; secured to the deck of the nearest vessel is engine No 2924, bound for an overseas port. This is a typical dockside scene, with a mixture of railway vans and wagons; the 12-ton Eastern Region van in the foreground is No E256202, while to the right are a mixture of three-, five- and seven-plank wagons. *Associated British Ports*

This vessel berthed at South Quay is discharging raw sugar into railway wagons in September 1933. The wagons seen nearest the camera are again GWR five-plank opens, while those behind are covered with LMS and LNER tarpaulins. The wagon partly seen on the left is a 12-ton Southern Railway vehicle. *Associated British Ports*

The New Zealand liner *Remvera*, built in 1911 and of 11,300 GRT, embarking passengers at South Quay in 1936. She was sunk off Kinnaird Head four years later in August 1940, probably by a German submarine. *Associated British Ports*

The SS *Seapool* at berth near No 6 transit shed at South Quay on 23 August 1950, taking aboard Austin motor cars, fitted with left-hand drive. The lifting technique in use by the crane nearest the camera can be seen to differ from the technique used behind. Pipes are being loaded aboard from former GWR 30 tons tare 'Macaw' bogie bolster wagons. Originally these wagons were built for the Taff Vale Railway, and in 1923 passed into GWR ownership. They were ideally suited for the carriage of wood, trees, telegraph poles and rails, as well as pipes. The example seen here is fitted with the updated type of oval buffers, while the original round buffers can be seen on the far wagon. Judging by the insignia on the ship's funnel, this vessel belongs to the Canadian Pacific Steamship Company. *Associated British Ports*

Right Cattle wagons discharging a shipment of bulls, en route to the Argentine, at South Quay in May 1952. This Hereford bull seems to be a little cautious about descending the ramp. The cage in front will be used to contain him as he is lifted aboard ship. The person on the ramp is holding a rope attached to a ring through the bull's nose, while the rest of the dockers look ready to flee if things don't go to plan! The van nearest the camera is a two-axle, 3-ton-load horse box van, numbered M42400. Also in the rake is another horse box and four passenger train cattle vans. *Associated British Ports*

Below This view of South Quay shows the storage area next to No 8 Transit Shed in September 1960. Alongside is moored the vessel *Egidia*, beneath the cranes are various types of iron ore hoppers, and in the foreground are a mixture of cars from the Austin factory. In the bottom left-hand corner is a 'frog-eye' Sprite, then an Austin Nash Metropolitan, unusual in having the spare wheel mounted on the rear, then a pair of Austin Cambridges – altogether a very good display of British-built cars en route to the American and Canadian markets. It is no wonder that the crane drivers are taking time off to watch their fellow dockers marshalling these cars into position – most people who worked on the docks could only afford push bikes in those days! *Associated British Ports*

Above The docks' former GWR 50-ton floating crane, assisted by the docks tug *Gwent*, is lifting railway coaches bound for the Indian Railways aboard the motor vessel *Indian Navigator*, of Calcutta, at its South Quay berth in October of 1954. *Associated British Ports*

Above right It is November 1956, and the Suez crisis has alarmed the Government of the day into action. At the South Quay berth the GWR-built 20-ton floating crane, working with the help of the docks tug *Newport*, is loading various War Department vehicles aboard the vessel *Framlington Court* en route to the Egyptian trouble spot. In the cradle sling of the floating crane can be seen a Scammell Explorer, while on deck are two AEC Matador four-wheelers; unseen, and also waiting their turn to be loaded, are six-wheeled AEC Militant vehicles and more Matadors, all en route to the Airborne Division. *Associated British Ports*

Cars for export being unloaded from railway vans via the unloading ramp at the end of a siding next to No 8 Transit Shed at South Quay circa 1952. The van is a GWR 'Python'-type covered carriage van. *Associated British Ports*

The Salvage Factory

About 1915 the railway lines leading to the south side of South Dock were extended to serve the newly built Salvage Factory, officially the Cartridge and Box Repair Works. Mainly staffed by women workers, it was used for the reconditioning of shell cases and ammunition boxes, as well as many other items that were returned from the battlefields of France and Belgium during the First World War. Later designated the National Box Repair Factory, it was bought from the War Department by the GWR under an agreement dated 21 November 1924. Because of the distance from the factory to the dock entrance, the ANDR provided a train service between the two points for the women workers as well as proposing a service to South Quay for general cargo workers in 1919.

The Cartridge and Box Repair Works, later known as the National Box Repair Factory, was bought by the GWR from the War Department in 1924, and the 486,800 square feet of floor space was sub-let for the storage and general handling of imports and exports. Today one-third of this factory area is owned by the firm of Bowater, the remainder becoming the new No 8 Transit Shed. This photograph shows the Factory's covered loading platform circa 1929. The dock gates platform can still be seen in Messrs Braithwaites works yard, which is now known as Rocord Limited. *Associated British Ports*

East Quay

This quay was built during 1904 and was situated, as its name suggests, on the east side of the South Dock; it was in use within that year, having a berth of 800 feet. By 1914 it was equipped with eight powerful hydraulic cranes; Nos 20, 22, 23, 24, 25 and 27 were of the movable type with luffing jibs and a lifting capacity of 3 tons 3 cwt, while numbers 21 and 26 were similar but lifted 3 tons and 6 tons when needed.

Also on this quay was a brick-built warehouse 200 feet long and 70 feet wide, the floor of which consisted of a platform for the under-cover loading and unloading of railway wagons; this platform projected from the warehouse, allowing easy handling of traffic between the building and the shipping at East Quay.

Right A sketch of SS *City of Paris* embarking passengers and loading general cargo while berthed at East Quay, South Dock, circa 1913. Note the temporary wooden-planked walkway across the railway lines, complete with handrails. *ANDR booklet of 1916*

Below American troops disembarking at East Quay at the end of the First World War, with a troop train waiting to take them away to the transit camps. In the foreground can be seen onlookers, possibly dockers, with more than one wishing that it was his son that was returning home. On the hull of the troopship can be seen the zigzag camouflage that was designed to break up a ship's outline. *Associated British Ports*

A large vessel at berth at East Quay Circa 1914. Three lines of tracks can be seen alongside the hydraulic cranes next to No 3 Transit Shed, as these warehouses were called by the GWR. On the right, suspended on a bracket, is a very good example of the early type of electric lights in use. Also in view are some GWR open plank wagons with one in the process of being unsheeted. *Associated British Ports*

Another sketch showing what could almost be a market scene, circa 1913. Actually it is prize-winning pedigree cattle, possibly Herefords, being shipped on to the SS *Spencer* en route to South America for breeding. *ANDR booklet of 1916*

In 1919 special passenger trains were run by the ANDR to East Quay to connect with vessels of the Royal Mail Company, especially the SS *Ebro*, which was a regular visitor to these docks. This photograph shows the passenger train on the left, with the *Ebro* at the quayside, taking on passengers en route for South America. Hydraulic crane number 23 is nearest the camera. *Associated British Ports*

This photograph was taken under wartime censorship controls, and shows an unidentified area of the Alexandra Docks, possibly East Quay, on 21 July 1945, shortly before the end of the Second World War. It shows a shipment of Valentine tanks awaiting dispatch aboard ship; as can be seen these were carried to Newport on LMS low-loading wagons from the Vickers Armstrong factory in Birmingham. Two years earlier these tanks would have been sent to Burma, but at this period in the war, having been surpassed by the British Churchill and the American Sherman tanks, they will possibly be on their way to Greece. They are in drab green, with no squadron markings. *Associated British Ports*

The northern section of East Quay, now known as Middle Quay, is the location of Nos 3 and 4 Transit Sheds. This photograph, taken on 17 June 1905, shows that the construction of Messrs Armstrong Whitworth's new hydraulic cranes is complete and they are ready for work. No 3 Transit Shed is half-completed. Until recently this part of Middle Quay handled banana traffic from Jamaica and other parts of the West Indies, and citrus fruits from Israel. *Associated British Ports*

The SS *River Afton* discharges iron ore via the travelling cranes at Middle Quay in March 1954. In the background is No 3 Transit Shed, with engine No 666, originally Alexandra Dock engine No 34, hauling the train. This 0-6-0 tank engine was built by Messrs Kerr Stuart and is seen here a short time before its withdrawal in 1955. *Associated British Ports*

North Quay

The ANDR booklet compiled by Mr Macaulay on 30 July 1906, which describes the work done on the South Dock extension, also contains a most descriptive study of the working arrangements as well as the structure of the docks' coaling hoists, and makes very interesting reading:

'The substructures of the coal tips already referred to will consist in each case of a massive tower of solid concrete, about 56 feet long by 35 feet wide, and will have a height of 56 feet, the foundation being carried down to the hard stratum, well below the level of the dock bottom, and the top rising to the quay level. The space intervening between the top of the tower and the edge of the dock slope is to be spanned by steel girders resting on intermediate brick piers and carrying a double line of rails on which the full wagons will be run to the cradle of the hoist.

'Above these girders and partly supported thereon, a viaduct of steel resting on trestles of the same materials will serve to convey the empty wagons to their respective sidings. Where the viaduct crosses the quay its trestles will be carried on substantial bases of brindle, brickwork and concrete, supported in case of any subsidence to the newly formed dock slope by whole timber pitch pine piles of great length driven to the hard sub stratum.

'Each coal hoist will be provided with a turntable and two weighbridges, one for the

The coal hoists at North Quay circa 1923 - that nearest the camera is No 18, followed by 17, 16, 15 and 14 in the distance. The vessel at number 18 hoist is the *City of Messina*, and judging by the amount of coal heaped above the hold the crew are hard at work shovelling to distribute this load evenly. On the left can be seen one of the open plank colliery wagons of the Tredegar Iron & Coal Company, from the Mclaren pits at New Tredegar. The motor car appears to be of 1920s vintage. *Associated British Ports*

Above Overlooking Alexandra Docks from the top of coaling hoist No 2, on the North Quay side of South Dock, in the background can be seen the coaling roads and coal wagons awaiting tipping, but unfortunately too far away to be identified. The date is 11 April 1916. *Associated British Ports*

Below The new transverser type of coal hoist under construction circa 1930. *Associated British Ports*

full, and one for the empty wagons. The full wagons will be run to the weighbridge down a "gravity" siding with carefully proportioned gradients, thence they will be drawn to the hoists by hydraulic power, hoisted, tipped, and returned over the viaduct to the empties siding, gravity being again the motive power. A total length of seven miles of gravity sidings will be provided, for the present, in addition to the line running alongside the dock.'

The types of cargo handled by these docks was quite varied and by 1904 consisted of general cargo, railway material, tin plate and corrugated tin, as well as coal. The latter was not only from the coalfields of the Rhondda, Aberdare and Merthyr areas, but also from the Forest of Dean and the Monmouthshire coalfields. It was brought into the docks by the Monmouthshire Railway & Canal Company as well as the ANDR's own PC&N line from Pontypridd.

The method of coal shipping at these docks was a combination of high and low level working:

'The wagon of coal is run from the sidings to the hoists at quay level, lifted to the necessary tipping height, and discharged, but instead of returning the empty wagon to the same level it is returned along a separate overhead way, carried on pillars to the hoists. Whilst the empty wagon is thus being dealt with, well away from the road for the full ones, the next full one is being brought to the cradle of the hoist, and when this has returned to ground level, the wagon is immediately run on, and the whole process repeated. It will thus be seen that the loading is practically a continuous cycle, limited solely by the use of anti-breakage boxes with the first portion of the cargo and the rate of "trimming" in the holds, and the handling of full and empty wagons, to and from the hoists.'

Before the decline of the coal exports from South Wales these docks contained a tremendous amount of siding accommodation, covering a total of 50 miles, with three low-level lines leading to each hoist. Vessels were loaded by day and night, and in 1901 Mr Macaulay directed that the old

GWR 20-ton coal wagons at No 20 coaling hoist, which was separate from the others, circa 1930. It was near this hoist that a proposed dry dock was to be constructed, situated at the bottom end of South Dock. Until 1990 this area was the reception point for Japanese cars being imported into Wales. With its three huge car terminals, this part of the docks was an ideal place to receive the NYK and Wallenius vessels that delivered the cars, as they could make maximum use of the constant water levels. *Associated British Ports*

charge of 1d per ton for the shipment of coal by night was to cease; although this meant the loss of extra revenue, it was a shrewd move as the extra shipments that followed tripled the revenue.

In 1914 the charges for the use of coal hoists were set at 2d per ton, and the weighing of coal or coke was 1 farthing per ton; for the shipment of stones by crane at the coal hoists a minimum charge of 2s 6d per hour was made.

For the lifting of cargoes weighing a total of 30 tons, the charges per lift were as follows: lifts not exceeding 3 tons, 3d per ton; 3 tons but not exceeding 5 tons, 1s 6d; rising to 6s 6d for a lift of 25 tons but not exceeding 30 tons.

Left This photograph shows the SS *Lake Clear*, an American vessel, wearing the zig-zag camouflage of the First World War, berthed alongside No 9 coaling hoist at North Quay on the north-west side of South Dock circa 1916. This hoist had a lift of 70 feet from quay level. *Associated British Ports*

Below At North Quay the vessel nearest the camera is the SS *Doric Star*, seen here after leaving its South Quay berth where it has taken on supplies; it is now at No 18 coaling hoist, taking on fuel. The other vessels at the quay are the *Cory Collier* at No 17 hoist, with *Turnbull Scott* at No 16, and the liner *Brocklebank* at No 14. The *Doric Star*, of 10,086 gross registered tons, was built in 1921; in December 1939 she was captured and sunk by the German pocket battleship *Graf Spee*. *Associated British Ports*

Bottom This scene from about 1923 gives one a good idea of the vastness of North Quay, with its extensive coal lines leading to the towering coal hoists. The photographer is facing north-east towards the Junction Cut direction; nearest the camera is hoist No 19, with Nos 18, 17, 16, 15 and 14 in that order beyond. To the left of hoist No 19, in the far distance, can be seen the coaling hoists of North Dock. The North Quay hoists eventually fell into disuse when the decision was made to transfer the coal trade of South Wales from Newport Docks to Barry and Swansea Docks instead, and the removal of the hoists and roads started in August 1964. While sad, it has to be admitted that to keep abreast of modern developments changes have to be made, and for the sake of the docks Newport had to change. By 1996 this area was covered by massive timber stocks, some stacked almost 20 feet high, supervised and controlled by the experienced staff of timber merchants MBM Ltd (Macmillan, Bloodel & Meyer), whose Forest Products Terminal is one of the largest of its type in Europe, handling products mainly from the forests of Canada. Sadly the stocks have since been removed from the quay. *Associated British Ports*

Above American-built tanks being discharged from a vessel at North Quay in April 1942. *Associated British Ports*

Right Increase of dock rates, dues and charges, 21 August 1918. *Associated British Ports*

COPY

ALEXANDRA (N. & S.W.) DOCKS AND RAILWAY.

NOTICE OF INCREASE OF DOCK RATES, DUES AND CHARGES

NOTICE IS HEREBY GIVEN that pursuant to power conferred on the Company by an Order of the Board of Trade dated the third day of June, 1918, the Alexandra (Newport & South Wales) Docks and Railway Company intend to increase the charges for tipping and weighing coal and coke by machinery to the sum of sixpence per ton and to increase all other Dock Statutory Rates Dues and Charges by Fifty per cent. Such increased rates dues and charges are to come into operation as from midnight of August 31st, 1918, and particulars of the same can be obtained at the Office of the Company, Newport, Mon.

BY ORDER,

J. H. VICKERY,

General Manager,

Alexandra(Newport & South Wales) Docks & Railway Company.

Newport, Mon.
August 31st, 1918.

Cranage facilities at Newport Docks

From 1898

Builder	Date built	Number and type	Scrapped
Armstrong Whitworth Co	1898	One: fixed, hydraulic, fixed jib, 30 ton lift	1963
Armstrong Whitworth Co	Unknown	Three: mobile, hydraulic, fixed jib, 2 ton lift	July 1959
Armstrong Whitworth Co	1905	Three: movable, hydraulic, fixed jib, one of 3 to 1½ ton lift, two of 6 to 3 ton lift	1957
East Ferry Road Engineering Co	1909	Nine: movable, hydraulic, luffing, 3 to 1½ ton lift	1957 (2), May 1960 (1), Sept 1959 (6)
East Ferry Road Engineering Co	1909	Three: movable, hydraulic, luffing, 6 and 4 to 2 ton lift	Sept 1959 (2), third transferred to Port Talbot Docks
Hydraulic Engineering Co	1914	Six: movable, hydraulic, luffing, 3 ton to 27 cwt lift	May 1960
Armstrong Whitworth Co	1918	Two: movable, hydraulic, luffing, one of 10 and 6½ to 3¼ ton lift, one of 6 and 4 to 2 ton lift	1957 (1), 1959 (1)
Stothert & Pitt Ltd	1925-31	22: portal, electric, luffing, 3 ton lift	Early to mid-1960s
GWR	1942-44	Four: portal, electric, luffing, 3 ton lift	1973-76
Stothert & Pitt Ltd	1927 (2), 1942 (1)	Three: portal, electric, level, luffing, 6 ton lift	1972
Clyde Engineering Co	1925-28	Three: portal electric, luffing 6 ton lift	1972
Stothert & Pitt Ltd	1950	One: portal, diesel-electric, luffing, 6 ton lift	
Stothert & Pitt Ltd	1959-60	Six: portal, electric, level, luffing, 3 ton lift	Early 1980s
Stothert & Pitt Ltd	1951	Four: portal, electric, level, luffing and grabbing, 11½ and 10 ton lift	1970s (2), remaining two refurbished in 1987 and still in use
Stothert & Pitt Ltd	1962-64	Five: portal, level, luffing and grabbing, 11½ and 10 ton lift	Mid-1980s (1), two refurbished in 1994, four still in use
Stothert & Pitt Ltd	1965	Two: portal, electric, level, luffing, 25 ton lift	Still in use
John Henderson & Co, Aberdeen	1969	One: electric derrick, 32 ton lift	1993
Paececo Vickers	1969	One: Portainer, 30 ton lift	Transferred to Hull Docks late 1970s
J. H. Wilson	1918	Four: steam travelling cranes, 10 ton lift	1961 (3), 1968 (1)
Grafton Engineering Co	1890	One: steam travelling crane, 5 ton lift	1968
Thomas Smith Rodley	1953	One: steam travelling crane, 10 ton lift	1980s
Thomas Smith Rodley	1963	One: diesel rail crane, 5 ton lift	1980s; donated to railway society

1995

Number	Lift (tons)	Remarks
13	6	
13	3	
6	11½	General cargo type
6	10	Grabbing cranes
1	10	General cargo type
1	8	Grabbing crane
2	25	John Boyd type
1	45	Mobile harbour crane, Mannesmann Demag Ltd
1	6	General cargo type
2	11½	General cargo type
1	10	General cargo type

Middle Quay, Fruit Terminal

Number	Lift (tons)	Remarks
3	6	General cargo type

South Quay, South Dock

Number	Lift (tons)	Remarks
3	6	General cargo type
4	10	Grabbing cranes
2	25	General cargo type
4	11½	General cargo type

Mobile cranes

Number	Lift (tons)	Remarks
1	45	General cargo type, Mannesmann Demag Ltd
1	20	Grabbing crane

2002

Number	Lift (tons)	Remarks
North side, South Dock		
2	10	Grabbing crane
1	8	Grabbing crane

Particulars of Hydraulic Cranes.

Where Situated.	Distinguishing No.	Type.	Lifting Capacity.	Radius Max.	Radius Min.	Rail level to underside of hook. Min.	Mix.	Man.	Total Lift.
South Dock Extension:—									
South Quay	32	Movable (with luffing jib)	3 t. & 30 c.	45'	27'		35' 9"	47' 0"	60'
"	33	"	6, 4 & 2 tons	45'	26'		32' 4"	44' 3"	60'
"	34, 35, 36	"	3 t. & 30 c.	45'	27'		35' 9"	47' 0"	60'
"	37	"	6, 4 & 2 tons	45'	26'		32' 4"	44' 3"	60'
"	38, 39, 40, 41	"	3 t. & 30 c.	45'	27'		35' 9"	47' 0"	60'
"	42	"	6, 4 & 2 tons	45'	26'		32' 4"	44' 3"	60'
"	43	"	3 t. & 30 c.	45'	27'		35' 9"	47' 0"	60'
" (44 to 51) 6 cranes		"	3 t. & 30 c.	50'	25'		36' 0"	36' 0"	60'
" 1 crane		"	6, 4 & 2 tons	50'	25'		36' 0"	36' 0"	60'
"	1	"	10, 6½, 3½ tons	50'	25'		36' 0"	36' 0"	60'
Town Dock Outer Basin:—									
East side	1	Movable (with fixed jib)	30 cwt.	25'	6"		24' 6"		48'
West side	2	Fixed	25 cwt.	28'	0"		26' 6"		36'
Inner Basin:—									
Junction	3	"	25 cwt.	26'	0"		25' 0"		40'
West side	4, 5	Movable	25 "	27'	6"		24' 0"		40'
"	6	Fixed	30	27'	0"		27' 6"		46'6"
Total	65 cranes								

Particulars of Hydraulic Cranes.

Where Situated.	Distinguishing No.	Type.	Lifting Capacity.	Radius.	Rail level to underside of hook.	Total Lift.
North Alexandra Dock:— Timber Stage	1, 2, 3	Movable (with fixed jib)	Tons 2	26' 6"	26' 9"	46'
"	4, 5, 6 and 7	"	2½	32' 0"	25' 0"	50'
"	8 and 9	"	2½	33' 0"	25' 0"	47'
East Quay	10	"	3	38' 6"	40' 0"	60'
"	11	"	6	42' 6"	36' 0"	60'
"	12	"	3	38' 6"	40' 0"	60'
"	13	"	6	42' 6"	42' 0"	60'
"	14, 15	"	3	42' 6"	40' 0"	60'
"	16	"	6	42' 6"	40' 6"	50'
"	17	Fixed (with fixed jib)	30	43' 0"	46' 6"	50'
"	18	"	2½	26' 6"	20' 6"	50'
"	19	"	2	28' 0"	22' 6"	60'
River Wharf	28	Movable (with fixed jib)	2	27' 0"	22' 6"	60'
"	29, 30	"	2	28' 0"	22' 6"	60'
"	31	"	2	27' 0"	22' 6"	60'
South Alexandra Dock:— East Quay	20	Movable (with luffing jib)	3 t. & 30 c.	45' 0"	44' 0"	60'
"	21	"	6 & 3 tons	45' 0"	44' 0"	60'
"	22, 23, 24, 25	"	3 t. & 30 c.	45' 0"	44' 0"	60'
"	26	"	6 & 3 tons	45' 0"	44' 0"	60'
"	27	"	3 t. & 30 c.	45' 0"	44' 0"	60'

From an ANDR booklet of 1914.

506   NEW—NEW   HAND-BOOK OF RAILWAY STATIONS, &c.

STATION ACCOMMODATION	CRANE POWER (Tons Cwts)	STATIONS, &c.	COUNTY	COMPANY	POSITION
G P		Newpark	Edinburgh (Col.)	L.M.S. (Col.)	Holytown and Edinburgh.
L H	1 10	Murieston Siding	Edinburgh	L.M.S. (Col.)	
P		New Park Pit	Yorks	L.N.E. (G.N.)	Same as Low Moor Ironworks Co. (Leeds). (Fencehouses.)
		New Penshaw Siding	Durham	L.N.E. (N.E.)	See London Brick Co. and Fordem, Ltd. (Peterboro')
		New Peterboro' Brick Sidings	Hunts	L.N.E. (G.N.)	
P	1 10	New Pool Colliery	Carmarth'	G.W. (B.P.G.V.)	Bury Port.
P		Newport	Essex	L.N.E. (G.E.)	Cambridge and Bishops Stortford.
		Barnard Bros.' Siding	Essex	L.N.E. (G.E.)	Newport.
L H	3 0	Wenn's, T. E., Siding	Essex	L.N.E. (G.E.)	Newport.
P		Newport	I. of W.	Southern (F.Y.N.); Southern (I.S.W.)	Cowes and Ryde. Newport Junction and Carisbrooke.
G	2 0	Gourville Siding	Mayo	G.S. (M.G.W.)	Steamer from Southampton. Carnisbrooke and Watchingrwll. Westport and Achill.
L H		NEWPORT—	Mon		
		Adams, A. R. & Son's Pill Dock ... S.Works	Mon	G.W.	Over Tredegar Estate Lines.
		Adams, W. & Co.	Mon	G.W. (A.D.R.-G.W.)	Pilgrimcly Coal Yard. Newport.
G	30 0	Alexandra Docks (GW ADR)	Mon	G.W. (A.D.R.-G.W.)	Branch from Dock Street
		Anglo-American Oil Co.'s Siding	Mon	G.W.	Liverpool Wharf.
		Arrol's (Sir Wm.), Ltd.	Mon	G.W.; G.W. (A.D.R.-G.W.)	Rhoswen Wharf. Alexandra Docks.
		Arrow Fuel Co.'s Works	Mon	G.W.	Over Tredegar Estate Lines.
		Bailey's, C. H, Engineering Works	Mon	G.W.	
		Bailey, C. H., Graham & Co.'s Dry Docks	Mon	G.W.	Alexandra Docks.
		Basic Slag & Phosphate Co.	Mon	G.W.	Garngetnin Wharf.
		Batchelor & Co.'s Timber Yd.	Mon	G.W.	Netsfold's Branch.
		Batchelor, T. B. & S., & Co. (Timber Importers)	Mon	(A.D.R.-G.W.)	Dock Street and Mill Street.
		Blns Street Timber Yd Sids.	Mon	G.W.	Town Dock.
		Bolt Street Timber Yd Side.	Mon	G.W.	Dock Street.
		Braithwaite & Co.'s Neptune Works	Mon	G.W.	Over Tredegar Estate Lines.
		British Mannesmann Tube Works Co., Ltd., Siding	Mon	G.W.	Branch from East Usk Junction.
		British Petroleum Co., Ltd. Sid. (Quiet/Wennn's Row)	Mon	G.W.	Branch from Dock Street
		Burt Boulton & Heywood's Timber Creosote Yard.	Mon	G.W. (A.D.R.-G.W.)	Alexandra Dock.
		BteWorks Supply Co.'s Sid	Mon	G.W. (A.D.R.-G.W.)	Alexandra Docks.
		Cambrian Wagon Co., Ltd.	Mon	G.W.	Dock Parade. Over Tredegar Estate Lines.
		Garngetnin Wharf,	Mon	G.W.	Town Dock.
		Cashmore, John,	Mon	G.W. (A.D.R.-G.W.)	Blaina Wharf.
		Siding	Mon	G.W.	Rhymney Wharf.
		Siding	Mon	G.W.	Russell's Wharf.
		Central Works,	Mon	G.W.	Dock Street and Mill Street.
		Cheshire, T., & Co.'s Warehouse	Mon	G.W. (A.D.R.-G.W.)	Alexandra Docks.
		Chiderhill Wharf	Mon	G.W.	Dock Street and Mill Street.
		Clapp's Wharf	Mon	G.W.	Town Dock.
		Clark, Geo., & Co.	Mon	G.W. (A.D.R.-G.W.)	East Usk Wharf.
		Clements, Chas., Ltd.	Mon	G.W.	East Usk Wharf.
		Collier, Chas., Ltd.	Mon	G.W.	Gloucester Wharf.
		Co-operative Wholesale Society Mills	Mon	G.W.	Herbert's Siding.
		Cordes, ..., Dos Works	Mon	G.W.	Town Dock.
		Corr. Electric Const. Yard	Mon	G.W. (A.D.R.-G.W.)	Branch near Dock Street.
		Courtybella Coal Yard (Jones, J., Rees & Co.)	Mon	G.W.	East Usk Wharf.
		Covenok Coal Yard (J. J. P. Ishit)	Mon	G.W.	Over Tredegar Estate Lines.
			Mon	G.W.	East Usk Wharf.

EXPLANATION—G Goods Station. P Passenger and Parcel Station. P* Passenger, but not Parcel or Miscellaneous Traffic. L Live Stock.
F Furniture Vans, Carriages, Portable Engines, and Machines on Wheels.
H Horse Boxes and Prize Cattle Vans. C Carriages by Passenger Train.

507   HAND-BOOK OF RAILWAY STATIONS, &c.   NEW—NEW

STATION ACCOMMODATION	CRANE POWER (Tons Cwts)	STATIONS, &c.	COUNTY	COMPANY	POSITIONS
		Newport—continued.			
		Davies, H., & Son (C. & A. Fontaine)	Mon	G.W.	East Usk Wharf.
		Dibble, J. O., & Co.	Mon	G.W.	Rock Wharf. Over Tredegar Estate Lines.
		Dock Foundry (C. & A. Fontaine)	Mon	G.W.	
		Dock Parade Sidings	Mon	G.W.	Over Tredegar Estate Lines. Ormbran and Waterloo Junction.
G	5 0	Dock Street (G. W.)	Mon	G.W.-B.&M.; L.M.S. (L.N.W.)	Over G. W. from Hereford. Over G. W. and Ormbran. High Street and Llanwern.
G F L		DocNailWorks (Cordnet Co.)	Mon	G.W.	High Street and Mill Street.
		East Usk Wharf (Great Western Wharf)	Mon	G.W.	
		Ebbw Vale Steel, Iron, and Coal Co.—	Mon		
		Ebbw Vale Iron Wharf	Mon	G.W.	Dock Street and Mill Street.
		Mariner's Wharf (Sleeper Plant Works)	Mon	G.W.	Dock Street and Mill Street.
		Pontypool Wharf	Mon	G.W.	Dock Street and Mill Street.
		Victoria Wharf (C. D. Phillips)	Mon	G.W.	Dock Street and Mill Street.
		Emlyn Foundry (C. D. Phillips)	Mon	G.W.	Dock Street and Ormbran.
		Evans, William, Grindan Glass Works (G. W.)	Mon	G.W.-L.M.S. (L.N.W.)	Ship Siding. Over Tredegar Estate
		Finlay Conveyor Co.'s	Mon	G.W.	East Usk Wharf.
		Bothdin Yard	Mon	G.W.	Loco. Yard, Dock Street.
		Fleming Composition Co.	Mon	G.W.	Gloucester Wharf.
		Fontaine's Foundry	Mon	G.W.	Dock Street and Ormbran.
		Ford & Pickford's Timber Yd	Mon	G.W.	Moderator Wharf.
		Fruit Distributing Co., Ltd.	Mon	G.W. (A.D.R.-G.W.)	Dock Street and Ormbran.
		Gas Works	Mon	G.W.	Llanarth Wharf.
		Gilchrist, R., & Co.'s Siding	Mon	G.W.	Dock Parade. Over Tredegar Estate Lines.
		Goss, A. J. T., & Co.	Mon	G.W.	Same as East Usk Wharf.
		Gould's Foundries, Ltd.	Mon	G.W.	Herbert's Siding.
		Great Western Wharf	Mon	G.W.	
		Greenland, G., & Son	Mon	G.W.	On East Usk Wharf (Great Western Wharf) Lines.
		Gwent Iron & Steel Wks	Mon	G.W.	Dock Street and Mill Street.
L H	8 0	Imperial Iron & Steel Co.	Mon		
L H		Patent Nut & Bolt Wharf	Mon	G.W.	Panner Wharf.
L H		Hall, Lewin, & Co.'s Wagon Works	Mon	G.W.	East Usk Wharf.
		Hardwick, William	Mon	G.W.	Pill Wharf.
		Harding, A.	Mon	G.W.	Branch from East Usk Junction.
		Healey & Feast, Ltd.	Mon	G.W.	High Street and Caerleon.
		Herbert's Siding	Mon	G.W.	Gloucester Wharf and Cardiff.
G F L		High Street (G. W.)	Mon	G.W. (B.&M.); L.M.S. (L.N.W.)	Over G. W. from Nine Mile Point Jn.
P		Hodge, Ralph, & Co.	Mon	G.W.	Lysaght & Co.'s Siding
P		Hodson & Concrete Products, Ltd.	Mon	G.W.	
		Houlder Bros. & Co.'s Warehouse	Mon	G.W. (A.D.R.-G.W.)	Alexandra Dock. King's Parade. Over Tredegar Estate Lines.
		International Bottle Glde. Co.	Mon	G.W.	Branch from Dock Street.
		Isca Foundry Co.	Mon	G.W.	East Usk Wharf.
		James & Emmanuel	Mon	G.W.	
		Jordan's Foundry (Pill Grenely Foundry).	Mon	G.W. (A.D.R.-G.W.)	Tillery Wharf.
		Lewis, E., Parade Sidings	Mon	G.W.	Town Dock.
		Lewis, C., & Co.	Mon	G.W.	Over Tredegar Estate Lines.
		Liverpool Wharf	Mon	G.W. (A.D.R.-G.W.)	Liverpool Wharf.
		Llanarth Street Electric Light Works	Mon	G.W.	Dock Street and Mill Street.
		Llanarth Wharf	Mon	G.W.	Town Dock.
		Lloyd, J., & Co.	Mon	G.W. (A.D.R.-G.W.)	Waterloo Wharf.
		Lysaght's Orb Iron Works	Mon	G.W.	Branch from East Usk Junction.
		Mahoney, J., & Co.	Mon	G.W.	King's Parade. Over Tredegar Estate Lines.

EXPLANATION—G Goods Station. P Passenger and Parcel Station. P* Passenger, but not Parcel or Miscellaneous Traffic.
F Furniture Vans, Carriages, Portable Engines, and Machines on Wheels. L Live Stock.
H Horse Boxes and Prize Cattle Vans. C Carriages by Passenger Train.

HAND-BOOK OF RAILWAY STATIONS, &c.

STATION ACCOMMODATION	CRANE POWER Tons	Cwts	STATIONS, &c.	COUNTY	COMPANY	POSITION
			NEWPORT—continued.			
			Mahoney, J. & Co.	Mon	G. W.	Town Dock.
			Maybury & Co.'s Kohla Works	Mon	G. W.	Clapp's Wharf.
			Maybury (Adamant and Plaster) Co.	Mon	G. W. (A.D.R.-G.W.)	Pill Wharf.
			Mandalgied Sidn (GW-ADR)	Mon	G. W. (A.D.R.-B.&M.)	Alexandra Docks.
			Mexico Oil & Grease Co.	Mon	G. W.	East Uak Wharf.
G.	10	0	Mill Street Mileage& Coal Sidings (G. W.)	Mon	(G. W.)(L.M.S.(L.N.W.))	Dock Street and Cwmbran. / Dock Street and Mill Street.
			Moderator Sidings	Mon	G. W.	Dock Street and Mill Street.
			Moderator Wharf	Mon	G. W.	Dock Street and Mill Street.
			Morris, H. & Co.'s Baltic Oil Works	Mon	G. W.	Town Dock.
			Morris, Wm., Ltd., Dock Parade Wagon Works	Mon	G. W.	Branch from Dock Street.
			Mount Stuart Dry Dock & Shearman's, Ltd.	Mon	G. W.	Ship Siding. Over Tredegar Estate Lines.
			Dry Dock Engineering Works.	Mon	G. W.	
			Dry Dock, West Side	Mon	G. W. (A. D. R.)	Alexandra Dock
			North Dock	Mon	G. W.	Branch from East Uak Junction.
			Eastern Dry Dock	Mon	G. W.	Dock Street and Mill Street.
			Siding	Mon	G. W.	Dock Street.
			Western Dry Dock	Mon	G. W.	
			Newport Enamel Slate Co. (Baker, W. A., & Co.)	Mon	G. W.	Caragthin Wharf.
			Newport Foundry	Mon	G. W.	Rock Wharf. Over Tredegar Estate Lines.
			Newport (Mon) Cold Storage and Ice Co., Ltd.	Mon	G. W.	
			Factory and Cold Stores	Mon	G. W. (A.D.R.-G.W.)	Alexandra Dock.
			Fish Wharf	Mon	G. W. (A.D.R.-G.W.)	Alexandra Dock.
			Nicholas & Co.'s Timber Yard	Mon	G. W.	Dock Street and Mill Street.
			Nicholas & Co.'s Timber Yard (Baltic Wharf)	Mon	G. W.	Waterloo Wharf.
			Parry, W. & Sons	Mon	G. W.	
			Partridge, Jones & John Paton's Pill Wharf (Newport Adamant & Plaster Co.)	Mon	G. W.	Branch near Dock Street.
			Penner Wharf	Mon	G. W.	Town Dock.
			Phillips & Son's Malt House	Mon	G. W.	Penner Wharf.
			Phillips, C. D.	Mon	G. W.	Central Iron Works.
			Pillgwenlly Coal Yard	Mon	G. W.	Branch from Dock Street.
			Pillgwenlly Foundry	Mon	G. W.	Branch from Dock Street.
			Pillgwenlly Wharf	Mon	G. W.	Over Tredegar Estate Lines.
			Powell's Town Wharf (Budd & Co.)	Mon	G. W.	Dock Street and Mill Street.
			Prothero's Wharf (G. P. Harding)	Mon	G. W.	Branch near Dock Street.
			Rees, F. J.	Mon	G. W.	Herbert's Siding.
			Rhewren Wharf	Mon	G. W.	Ship Siding. Over Tredegar Estate Lines.
			Rumney Wharf	Mon	G. W.	Town Dock.
			Rigley,W.&Co.'sWagon Wks	Mon	G. W. (A.D.R.-G.W.)	Vipond's Wharf.
			Risca Wharf	Mon	G. W.	Branch from Dock Street.
			River Coal Shipping Jetties	Mon	G. W. (A.D.R.-G.W.)	Alexandra Dock.
			Russell's Wharf	Mon	G. W.	Over Tredegar Estate Lines.
			Sessions & Sons	Mon	G. W. (A.D.R.-G.W.)	East Uak Wharf.
			Shell Mex, Ltd., Oil Depôt.	Mon	G. W.	Town Dock.
			Ship Siding	Mon	G. W.	Town Dock.
			Smith's (Newport) Ltd. Star Flour Mills	Mon	G. W.	Cinderhill Wharf.
			South Wales Malleable Iron Foundry (Keeley & Pearl)	Mon	G. W.	Branch from East Uak Junction.
			Spitzle, Thos., Ltd. (Cambrian Foundry)	Mon	G. W. (A.D.R.-G.W.)	Town Dock.
			Thomas, A.	Mon	G. W.	Waterloo Wharf.
			Tillery Wharf	Mon	G. W.	Town Dock.

EXPLANATION—G Goods Station.   P Passenger and Parcel Station.   P* Passenger, but not Parcel or Miscellaneous Traffic.   L Live Stock.
F Furniture Vans, Carriages, Portable Engines, and Machines on Wheels.
H Horse Boxes and Prize Cattle Vans.   C Carriages by Passenger Train.

HAND-BOOK OF RAILWAY STATIONS, &c.

STATION ACCOMMODATION	CRANE POWER Tons	Cwts	STATIONS, &c.	COUNTY	COMPANY	POSITION
			NEWPORT—continued.			
			Town Dock			
			Tredegar Dry Dock & Wharf	Mon	G. W. (A.D.R.-G.W.)	Branch from Dock Street.
			Siding	Mon	G. W.	Over Tredegar Estate Lines.
			Siding	Mon	G. W.	Branch from East Uak Station.
			Tredegar Estate Lines	Mon	G. W.	Branch near Dock Street.
			Trott, J. & Son	Mon	G. W.	Tillery Wharf.
			Uskside Engineering Co.			
			Vipond, J. & Co.		G. W.	Branch near Dock Street.
			Vipond's Wharf		G. W.	Vipond's Wharf.
			Vipond's Wharf		G. W.	Dock Street and Mill Street.
			Wagon Repairs, Ltd.—			
			Siding	Mon	G. W. (G.W.-A.D.R.)	King's Parade. Over Tredegar Estate Lines.
			Siding	Mon	G. W.	Town Dock.
			Walker Bros.	Mon	G. W.	Rieca Wharf.
			Waterloo Wharf	Mon	G. W.	Ship Siding. Over Tredegar Estate Lines.
			Western Navigation Co. Ltd	Mon	G. W.	East Uak Branch.
G.	5	0	Whitehead Iron and Steel Co., Ltd. Sid.(Courtybella)	Mon	G. W.	Dock Street and Maesglas Junction.
G. P.	2	0	Williams & Thomas	Mon	G. W.	East Uak Wharf.
G. P.			Newport	Salop	L.M.S.(L.N.W.)	Shrewsbury and Stafford.
G. P.			Newport	Yorks	L.N.E.(N.E.)	Stockton and Middlesbrough.
P			Newport	Fife	L.N.E.(N.B.)	Dundee and Tayport.
			Newport (East)	Fife	L.N.E.(N.B.)	Newport (East) and Tayport.
P			Newport (West)	Fife	L.N.E.(N.B.)	Dundee and Tayport.
			Newport Adamant & Plaster Co.	Mon		Saae as Partridge, Jones and John Paton, Ltd., Pill Wharf (Newport).
			Newport Enamel Slate Co. (Baker, W. A., & Co.)	Mon		Newport.
			Newport Engine Sheds	Yorks	L.N.E.(N.E.)	Middlesbrough.
			Newport Foundry Co.	Mon		Newport.
	5	0	Newport Iron Works, Coke Ovens and Wharf	Yorks	L.N.E.(N.E.)	Middlesbrough.
			Newport (Mon) Cold Storage and Ice Co., Ltd.—			
			Factory and Cold Stores	Mon	G. W. (A.D.R.-G.W.)	Newport, Alexandra Dock.
			Fish Wharf	Mon	G. W. (A.D.R.-G.W.)	Newport, Town Dock.
G. P. F. L. H. C	6	0	Newport Pagnell	Bucks	L.M.S.(L.N.W.)	Branch from Wolverton.
			Newport Pagnell Gas Works Coies & Son's Shipley Wharf	Bucks		Newport Pagnell and Great Linford.
			Price's Siding	Bucks	L.M.S.(L.N.W.)	Newport Pagnell.
			Newport River Co., Ltd.	Mon	G. W. (T. V.)	Elsworry.
			Newport Road Sidings	Glamorg'n	L.M.S.(L.N.W.)	See Cardiff.
			Newport Wire Works	Midd'sex		Southall.
			Newquay	Cornwall	G. W.	Branch from Par.
			British Petroleum Co., Ltd.	Cornwall	G. W.	Quintrell Downs Siding.
			Newquay Harbour	Cornwall	G. W.	Extension from Newquay.
G			Pollard's Siding	Cornwall	G. W.	Extension from Newquay.
			Quintrell Downs Siding	Cornwall	G. W.	Newquay and St. Columb Road.
			Stephens & Co.	Cornwall	G. W.	Quintrell Downs Siding.
			Trefemper Siding	Cornwall	G. W.	Tolcarn Junc. and Shepherd's Siding.
			New Quays	Devon	Southern (L.S.W.)	Devonport.
	1	0	New Radnor	Radnor	S. & D. Jt.	Branch from Tilley.
			New Romney & Littlestone	Kent	Southern (S. E. C) Southern (S. E. C) R. H. & D	Branch—Lydd and Dungeness. / Lermains.
	3	0	New Ross Vale Brick & Tile Co.'s Siding			Chesterton.
G. P. F. L. H.			New Ross	Staffs	L.M.S.(L.N.W.)	Maxnine Junction and Waterford.
G. P. F. L.			New Rufford Colliery	Kilkenny	G. S. (S. D.S.)	See Boisover Col. Co. (Blidworth).
			Newry—	Notts	L.M.S.(Mid.)	
G.			Albert Basin	Down	B. & Newry	Adjoining G. N. (I.) Station.
G.			Bridge Street	Armagh	D. N. & G.	Branch from King Street Junction.
G.	8	0	Bridge Street Junction	Armagh	D. N. & G. G. N. (I.)	Bridge Street Junction and Greenore.
G.			Carvill Bros. Siding	Down	G. N. (I.)	Edward Street and Warrenpoint.
G.	5	0	Dublin Bridge	Armagh	(G.N.) D. N. & G.	Gough Wood and Warrenpoint. / Over G. N. (I.) from Bridge Str. Jn.
G. P. F. L. H. C			Edward Street (G. N. (I.))	Down	L.N.E.(G. N. of S.)	Over G. N. (I.) from Bridge Str. Jn.
G. P.			Newseat	Aberdeen		Maud and Peterhead.

EXPLANATION—G Goods Station.   P Passenger and Parcel Station.   P* Passenger, but not Parcel or Miscellaneous Traffic.   L Live Stock.
F Furniture Vans, Carriages, Portable Engines, and Machines on Wheels.
H Horse Boxes and Prize Cattle Vans.   C Carriages by Passenger Train.

Extracts from the Railway Clearing House (RCH) *Hand-book of Railway Stations*, circa 1929, showing the vast number of private and company wharves and sidings in and around the docks at Newport. *Courtesy Mr D. C. Sims, Newport Harbour Commissioners Office*

An aerial view giving a clear indication of the position of Alexandra Docks. The River Usk winds its way past the town of Newport, which is situated to the left of the Transporter Bridge (top left of the picture at the base of the first bend of the river); on the right-hand side at the mouth of the Usk are the private Mountstuart Dry Docks. In the centre left of the photograph is North Dock, while the River Ebbw is seen in the bottom left-hand corner.

South Dock is in the centre of the photograph, with the piers of South Lock reaching out like feelers into the Bristol Channel; the west pier is on the left. Between the outer and inner gates of the lock can be seen the brick-built South Lock Power Station, which accommodated an economiser, water softening and feed pump house in one building, and in the other pumping, electric lighting and power house. The most prominent feature is the chimney stack, 187 feet high.

This 1935 photograph was duplicated and issued along with others to the German Luftwaffe bombing crews during 1940-42, the only difference being that compass points were superimposed. The photographs were collected after their briefings by the crews together with detailed written instructions in the correct folder for the area they were bombing; the Newport Docks folder was numbered GB7, BB27, number 2. The idea was that if the aircraft overshot their target they would fly onwards to the next one and use their bombs on that; for example, the next targets might be GB7, BB27 number 13, Messrs J. Lysaght Limited, steelworks; GB7, BB27 number 16, British Aluminium Company Works; and if not them, then GB7, BB27, number 61, the Neptune Machine Works.

The crews were also issued with a booklet of key installations that they could blow up, acting as saboteurs, if they were shot down. Many Germans posing as tourists took scenic photographs around England and Wales before the Second World War, and key installations would be included in the background. These 'holiday snaps' were then enlarged, ready for issue when war broke out. *Associated British Ports*

Disaster and heroism

Disaster struck on 2 July 1909 when a team of 53 men and boys employed as navvies and timbermen were working in the outer wall trench of the south-west wing of part of the new South Dock. At approximately 5.20pm, a matter of minutes before the end of their shift, a tremendous cracking sound was heard coming from the huge support timbers, and within a few seconds they were catapulted into the air before falling into the trench and on to the men 50 feet below. Only one man was visible amongst the debris of fallen timbers, earth, wagons and steam cranes – it was as if the earth had just opened up, one eyewitness stated.

Immediately the cave-in was heard, railway engines all over the extension workings began to sound their whistles to summon help, and within minutes rescuers had arrived and the operation to save those trapped was under way. However, the collapse was of a colossal scale, and time was against the rescuers.

The first immediate danger was from the collapsed steam cranes, which still had their boilers lit. Unless those fires were extinguished the men entombed beneath the twisted and mangled timbers would be burned to death.

A hero of the disaster was Thomas Lewis, a young lad of 14; he was a newspaper boy whose father worked on the docks as a stevedore. The noise of the steam whistles seemed to carry for miles, and Wallis Street, where Thomas lived, was like many other streets near the docks soon filled with talk of the disaster.

An injured man was found alive amongst the wreckage of broken beams and twisted metal, but the hole to reach him was narrow, too narrow for the broad-shouldered men of the rescue teams.

The collapsed trench, seen here on 4 July 1909, two days after the disaster, looking northwards. In view are some of the ANDR managers and members of the Board of Inspectors. The gentleman to the left of the group of four is Mr Macaulay, ANDR General Manager – he appears to be wiping his face. At the far end of the trench is what appears to be a cameraman and possibly members of the press. In the middle distance can be seen one of the contractors' engines with a short-wheelbase carriage attached, probably for the use of the Inspectorate. *Newport Resource Centre*

Above Another view of the disaster area, on 5 July 1909. The tidal water has flooded the collapsed workings. *Associated British Ports*

Below By 6 July the work to fill in the collapse is still in operation. The contractors' side-tip wagons and rotary cement mixer can be clearly seen. A large amount of water is still visible. *Associated British Ports*

Thomas Lewis, the boy hero of this terrible disaster. When hope was still fresh in the hearts of those whose men and sons were trapped, this lad risked his life to try and save them, being at the time only 14 years of age. Photographed here at the disaster area on 4 July 1909, he died in April 1969. *Newport Resource Centre*

Young Thomas went down, twisting his body as he worked his way through the fissure, crawling inch by inch until he finally reached the trapped man. With an effort in that maze of timber he started to free him, but before he was able to lead him to safety another fall started. With timbers starting to move it was all Thomas could do to scramble back upwards to safety before the narrow gap collapsed.

As darkness fell that night, hundreds of townsfolk watched as 500 men worked under the light of scores of acetylene flares, struggling, wrestling and heaving at the fallen 14-inch-thick timber mainstays and the 12-inch-thick cross-pieces, broken and twisted by the force that had caused their collapse.

Rescue operations continued throughout the night into Saturday 3 July, but by noon there was very little hope of anyone buried still being alive, and by the afternoon the tidal water began to seep over the excavated ground and eventually enter the collapsed trench. The teams had managed to recover five bodies and rescue 15 men, alive but injured; one of these later died from his injuries.

The next day, Sunday 4 July, the collapsed trench was full of water, and with the approval of the coroner work began immediately to fill it in. On 8 July a funeral service was held on the site of the disaster, attended by over 2,000 mourners, friends and families that had waited in vain. By 10 July the filling in of the trench was completed.

A year later, in December 1910, while work was under way to sink blocks of stone near the area of the disaster, a further 17 bodies were removed, leaving 16 still buried beneath the South Dock.

As a mark of his heroism Thomas Lewis was invited to tea at Buckingham Palace, and while there he was awarded the Albert Medal, Britain's highest award for civilian bravery in peace-time. The inscription reads 'For Gallantry in saving life on land'.

In the cemetery of St Woolos Church, Newport, is a monument to the dead, erected by Messrs Easton Gibb & Son, carrying a plaque that reads quite simply: 'As a tribute of respect to the memory of those 39 workmen who lost their lives in the trench disaster at the new dock works on the 2nd July 1909.'

The South Dock today

As mentioned in the Introduction, the Middle Quay has now ceased to be used as the Jamaica banana terminal. This quay is the site of Nos 3 and 4 Transit Sheds, both of which are equipped with specialised temperature controllers to protect the freshness of any fruit that may be stored there in the future. At present the outside storage area of this quay is being used for the stacking and storage of kiln-dried timber from the Riga area of Latvia.

Today's dockside road and rail traffic passes over the filled-in part of the former East Lock, and what is left is a quiet area of water for the mooring of smaller type of river craft. Located a short distance from here is the HM Customs & Excise building.

The Cement Terminal, on the south-east side of

South Dock, is located between the former East Lock and South Quay. Although the silos and buildings used by the Rugby Cement Company are at present disused, it is hoped that they will soon be back in operation.

On the opposite side of East Way Road is the designated coal storage area, the site of the former No 9 Shed, now long gone. This coal handling and washing area is situated well away from the docks' other activities.

South Quay is possibly one of the most important in the docks. With rail facilities reaching on to the quayside area, it is still the main embarkation point for rail traffic overseas. The former GWR Transit Shed No 5 and the new No 5A are located here, at present housing steel coils and tinplate from Turkey and Poland. Located west of No 5 is No 6 Transit Shed, also holding imported steel, and next to it is the No 7 Shed, built to house steel for export abroad; these new sheds replace the original Nos 7 and 8 Sheds, which have long since been demolished. Because rail traffic from this quay has direct access via the now much upgraded internal lines system, glass, containers, steel coils and rods, aluminium, as well as general types of cargo, can be hauled not only to other parts of South Wales and the Midlands, but also via the Channel Tunnel to and from the Continent.

The coal storage area of South Quay is used for the unloading of bulk shipments of mineral traffic, temporarily stored at the quayside coal storage area. This mostly consists of anthracite, coal and coke from Poland and other countries; during my visit the bulk carrier vessel *Murmansk*, of Valletta, was at the quayside. Once unloaded, the coal is separated from other materials, such as wood, by high concrete blocks; Associated British Ports has found it necessary to remove large stocks of timber that had previously been stored near these blocks due to the discovery of possible contamination by coal dust. To minimise coal handling time, this part of the quay is equipped with four 10-ton-capacity grabbing cranes, backed up by a 45-tonne Mannesmann Demag mobile crane equipped with a 16-tonne grab capacity.

This coal storage yard is on the site of the former Nos 7 and 8 GWR Transit Sheds, and nearby is the former Box Factory, complete with its covered loading bay, corrugated roof and cement walls.

Now in a very neglected state, it is due for demolition; at present it serves as a storage area, but one cannot help but think that it is strangely out of place in the docks today.

Between the coal storage area and the South Lock's inner entrance are two 6-tonne Revcon cranes, Nos 88 and 89, now disused and awaiting the dismantler's torch.

Across East Way Road is the No 8 Shed; located in part of the former Bowater premises, it is still in use housing timber and plywood. Next is the timber firm Norbulk, with such a large yard area that there is no problem with regard to storage of its timber imported from South America and the Far East, as well as from Russia, the Baltic states, Norway and other Scandinavian countries. A short distance from Norbulk, and also formerly part of the Bowater group premises, is the firm of SCA Packaging, which includes a moulded products building and a corrugated case plant; access is gained directly into these buildings from East Way Road.

At the lower east corner of North Quay, South Dock, is the Metal Reprocessing Terminal, handling various scrap metal imports; at the time of my visit I watched with interest the vessel *Vera*, from Willemstad, discharging her cargo of scrap metal at this berth. The north side of North Quay is spacious, and with the recent loss of MBM Limited and its Canadian timber, it is now used for the discharging of container and bulk cargo vessels. Four new sheds have been erected, far enough from the quayside to allow plenty of storage space. When I visited this part of the docks the eastern part was being used for the storage of steel girders, while in the central area mobile dust-suppressing hoppers were in constant use, while bulk aggregate, discharged by crane-operated grabs, was being lifted out of a cargo carrier's hold to be released into the top of the hoppers and through them into the road transport waiting underneath. This is a daily routine, and the vessel I saw being unloaded was the bulk carrier *Novigrad*, of Zadar, being served by one 8-tonne and two 10-tonne cranes. Also on standby was the 45-tonne harbour mobile crane, with its 16-tonne grab capacity.

Housing the other types of cargo that are discharged here are Nos 9 and 9A Sheds, which house imported fertiliser for the Iaws Fertiliser

Company. Shed No 10 is used for the storage of plywood and steel products, while No 11 houses imported raw products for use as animal feed, such as palm kernel, sunflower seeds and soya beans.

All along the south-west side of South Dock, almost reaching from the west side of the entrance into South Lock to the area of North Quay, is ground owned by the docks but designated for open storage, ready for leasing to any potential customer at a reasonable rate.

In the north-west corner, also close to North Quay, is the former car terminal area. This is at present unused, as are parts of North Quay, but Associated British Ports is hopeful of occupation, perhaps during 2002. This area is easily reached by a spur from West Way Road, and when occupied by Colt cars it had a waxing facility. Of the 18-hectare area, 6 were tarmac surfaced, while the remainder was given a surface of stone and shale, but at present only weeds stand here.

This photograph, taken on 27 July 2001 from alongside the South Lock entrance to South Dock, shows the vessel *Novigrad*, of Zadar, at North Quay, discharging her bulk cargo, while on the right *Murmansk*, of Valletta, is at the coal storage area of South Dock. The two Rev Con cranes, numbered 88 and 89, are disused and await the cutting torch. *Author*

3. THE TOWN DOCK

The Town Dock, or Old Dock as it was generally known, was situated in the town of Newport, a mile or so up the River Usk from the Alexandra Docks. Authorised by an Act of 1835, it was opened for trade on 10 October 1842, at a cost of £195,000. An extension under the Newport Dock Company Act of 1854 was completed and opened on 2 March 1858. These docks became the oldest property of the Alexandra (Newport & South Wales) Docks & Railway Company on 1 January 1884.

As in the case of the Alexandra North and South Docks, one side of the docks was devoted to coal shipping, while the other handled imports and general exports. The total area covered by the

Map of the Old, or Town, Dock at Newport, November 1907. *Cardiff Public Library*

docks was 11½ acres, with the total length of 1,753 feet and a width of some 300 feet. The depth of water was about 5 feet less than the Alexandra Docks.

The trade from the Town Dock was mainly in timber, with the whole of one end laid out as a timber slipway. Other shipments consisted of grain, hay and potatoes; this type of cargo suited the various types of smaller vessels that used these docks; the cargo was worked aboard by the crews themselves.

The first dock to be entered, that opened in 1842, was known as the Outer Basin, and covered an area of 4 acres. For 12 years this dock met the requirements of the town, before the 7½-acre extension of 1858 was opened; this was badly needed as annual shipments had risen to 250,000 tons and were rising steadily. The extension was named the Inner Basin. Designed by Mr Abernethy MInstCE and constructed by the firm of Messrs Rennie & Logan at a cost of £64,000, it was 1,000 feet in length and 400 feet wide.

In 1882 two vessels became jammed in the lock, remaining there for two weeks before being freed, and trapping 65 other ships in the docks. One wonders if subsequent claims by ship-owners for this delay to their vessels placed such a financial burden on the docks company as to contribute to the 1884 merger with the ANDR.

The Town Dock boasted an assortment of hydraulic cranes. No 1, on the east side, was of the movable type with a fixed jib and a lifting capacity of 30cwt, while on the west side was crane No 2; this was of the fixed type, and capable of lifting a maximum of 25cwt. At the junction of the Inner Basin was crane No 3, again a fixed type with a maximum lift of 25cwt. Crane No 4 was located on the west side of the Inner Basin, and was fixed with a lifting capacity also of 25cwt. No 5 was a movable crane, also with a lifting capacity of 25cwt, and finally there was No 6, of the fixed type but with a lifting capacity of 30cwt.

The Hydraulic Generating Power Station that served the Town Dock was finally abandoned in 1902, when hydraulic power was supplied via one of the three power stations at the Alexandra North Dock. By 1904 plans were being laid to reduce these three power stations to one, which would have the generating capacity of all three; this was to be situated at the north end of the North Dock.

By 1914 the Town Dock was equipped with four coal hoists, three being made out of steel and having a lift of 35 feet above quay level. These were designed to deal with loaded coal wagons of 23 tons gross weight.

The Town Dock was finally closed on 11 October 1930, when the gates were fixed open and it became tidal only, and used only at the user's risk. The *GWR Magazine* of 1939 stated: 'The

A sketch drawn by Mr J. F. Mullock circa 1842 showing Newport's Town Dock, with St Woolos Church in the far distance. On the day of opening the vessels along the wharves were decked in streams of bunting, and flags were hung across the streets from public as well as private buildings in the town. *Associated British Ports*

work in connection with the diversion of the Town Dock Feeder to the Alexandra Docks has been completed, and the water has been diverted. The old feeder, which passed under part of the town, has been filled in with sand to prevent collapse. The filling in of the Outer Basin has commenced, a stone block dam having been constructed across the entrance.'

The Blaina Wharf

This wharf, which adjoined the Town Dock, was also taken over by the ANDR in 1884. By 1904 it accommodated three hydraulic cranes with a lifting capacity of 2 tons, ideally suited for vessels built to carry 3,000-ton cargoes. Up to 1904 this wharf was notable in its handling of iron ore, which was discharged here en route to the furnaces of South Wales, usually the Blaenavon works.

The Town Dock today

By the 1990s all trace of the Town Dock had disappeared and the site had been filled in and grassed over; only the Outer Lock with the old malt warehouse nearby showed what had once been here. When I last saw the old lock, nearly six years ago, it was strewn with rubbish and dotted with the occasional supermarket trolley half submerged in the thick River Usk mud, so it was with some trepidation that I returned in July 2001. However, with backing from the Town Council changes have certainly been made, and the lock has been transformed. It is a credit to all of those concerned, for it must have taken no small effort by many people to achieve the present-day aspect. The lock is now surrounded by a newly laid walkway, young saplings have been planted at regular intervals, a bollard-type fence now skirts the edge of the lock wall, and even the dressed stone of this wall is clean. Decorative pillars are joined together by a single white chain, and the original lockside mooring buoys are freshly painted. In the lock itself, instead of water and mud there now grows tall lush grass. This has been an achievement of which local residents can feel rightly proud.

The Inner Lock area is also no longer the waste ground it once was. Weeds and rubble have been replaced by pathways, trees and cut grass, making this former neglected and abandoned area a pleasant place for children to play and dogs to exercise. Many towns have little or no grassed areas, as most have been built upon, so hopefully this area will stay green and perhaps one day become a designated park.

The Baltic Oil & Grease Company building is the former Alexandra (Newport) Docks wagon repair shop, and is as much a part of the history of Newport as the transporter bridge or the River Usk itself, just a short walk away. The first striking feature of this preserved building is its large cast iron doors, above which a cast iron plinth is dated 1844. Inside the imposing building are numerous cast iron pillars supporting the upper floors. Mr Stephen Meredith, the proprietor, kindly showed me into his office, and I was amazed to see that the original writing desk, probably of GWR origin, but possibly earlier, was still in use. Outside, along one side wall, four oil tank wagons straddle the short spur of this former docks line, leading in the direction of the docks, only to end abruptly at the perimeter fence. It is hard to believe that when these premises were built the Outer Basin of the Old Town Dock was a mere two years old.

The Entrance Lock that led into the Town Dock was 220 feet long and 61 feet wide; the depth of water to the entrance gates was 31 feet during average spring tides, reaching a depth of 36 feet during extraordinary spring tides. This early photograph, taken circa 1872 from the River Usk, shows the lock on the left, while on the extreme right is Penners Wharf.
Associated British Ports

Above This scene shows the Outer Dock in 1910, with vessels in the background at anchor in the Inner Basin. It was at these docks, up to 1904, that the short-wheelbase 0-4-0 engines Active, Alexandra and Trojan worked. *ANDR booklet of 1916, Newport Harbour Commissioners Office*

Below The Monmouthshire Railway & Canal Company yard at the Town Dock, circa 1872. The sailing vessels were known as 'luggers', and were used for coastal trading between Newport and Bristol. *Associated British Ports*

Left A captured German submarine, *UB91*, at anchor at the north end of the Inner Basin during an inspection by Naval officers from the Admiralty circa 1916. Shortly after this visit the submarine was put on open display to the public, and a notice placed on the shed on the right stated that admission was 1 shilling. *Associated British Ports*

Left A view of the Inner Basin circa 1917, photographed from the lock gates that separated the Inner and Outer docks. On the right is one of the steam coastal vessels of the type that made frequent use of these docks. *Associated British Ports*

Below The Baltic Oil & Grease Company building, seen in July 2001, was once the ANDR wagon repair workshops. The cast iron plinth above the doorway is dated 1844. *Author*

4. THE PC&N: PONTYPRIDD TO PENRHOS

Almost all of the railway companies that operated in South Wales had their own marked individuality and variety, and the PC&N line was no different. The following photographs show a varied selection of the types of engines used, the coaching stock, most of which was second-hand, and the closeness of part of the line to the Glamorganshire Canal, providing a rather picturesque setting. Variety was also provided by the other independent railway companies that came into daily contact with the PC&N as it travelled onwards towards its goal, the ANDR's Alexandra Docks complex.

The need for an independent line of railway was urgently discussed between Sir George Elliot and Lord Tredegar during the Alexandra Docks Company's board meeting on 16 July 1877. The conclusion was that a short line running between the town of Pontypridd and Caerphilly was needed as a connecting link to give the town of Newport and the Alexandra Docks direct and independent communication with the valleys of Aberdare and the Rhondda; also, the increase in coal traffic via the Tredegar Park Mile into the docks would increase the profits and royalties paid to Lord Tredegar and the other shareholders.

During the remaining part of 1877 Mr David Davies, MP and colliery owner, offered financial help with the building of the line, but later withdrew his offer. Perhaps he had other matters on his mind - the building of a railway line to the town of Barry, maybe.

On 29 November, on behalf of the ANDR, Mr Parkinson held a series of public meetings in the districts that would be affected by the proposed new railway line. The full reports that appeared in all the local newspapers must have caused quite a stir. It had been decided that land would have to

be purchased of sufficient width to allow for the building of a double line, and not a single line as was at first thought.

Mr Parkinson had already reported to the board on 20 June that the earnings of the Alexandra Docks had shown a gratifying increase from the year before. However, a careful analysis by Sir George Elliot convinced not only himself but also the board that until the railway rates between the South Wales coalfields and Newport were made equal with the rates of those coalfields and Cardiff, the earnings of the Alexandra Docks would only be made secure if the coal traffic from the South Wales coalfields went to Newport via the proposed Pontypridd and Caerphilly railway line into the Alexandra Docks. Thus the Pontypridd, Caerphilly & Newport Railway Company was born, incorporated by an Act of Parliament on 8 August 1878. Engineered by Mr J. W. Szlumper, the line was double-tracked as far as the Rhymney connection.

The line opened to coal traffic on 7 July 1884. The coal trains were manned 'with agreement' by the drivers and staff of the Taff Vale Railway from that date, until the agreement was discontinued, at the TVR's request, some 22 years later.

As fortune would have it, at that time the Mersey Railway Company had some unwanted engines for sale, and as the ANDR wanted to replace the original engines that had been used by the TVR on the coal traffic, ten were purchased for use on the coal trains from the Rhondda to Newport Docks, but this time operated by ANDR crews. This situation came into effect from 30 April 1906 and lasted until the railway grouping Act of 1922 came into force, when all trains were handled by the newly re-formed Great Western Railway (often using the same men).

TREFOREST.

THE PONTYPRIDD AND CAERPHILLY RAILWAY is now being proceeded with in real earnestness. We saw there a large number of trucks, planks, and other appliances for the work. There is also a host of navvies, masons, &c., busily engaged on the line. It is quite a new life in Treforest, this week the countenance of the sons of toil evidently indicating a cheerful heart. The trade of the neighbourhood will reap the benefit of these fresh tokens of revival. On Tuesday Mr Mackay, the well-known contractor, with his principal officials, accompanied by Mr Aitken and Mr Ogden, Cardiff, and a number of labourers, in charge of the necessary implements, arrived at Treforest for the purpose of proceeding with the above railway. The first sod was cut on the field near the Glyntaff Vicarage by Mr Aitken, Cardiff. The visitors afterwards went to the Llanbradach Hotel, where champagne was quaffed in honour of the event.

NEW RAILWAYS.—The operations in connection with the line from Pontypridd to Newport via Caerphilly are being carried out with the utmost vigour, under the conductorship of Mr Mackay, Newport, Mon. At a spot midway between here and Treforest on the Pentrebach road, a small mountain of hard stone is being removed by means of the powder blasting process, and men are employed day and night to hasten its completion, the stone produced being intended for the construction of a viaduct of several spans to cross the river Taff. Behind the Glyntaff church and vicarage at the other side of this large amount of stone and where the "navvies" are comparatively uninterrupted owing to the ground being level and loamy. Most marked progress has been made and we may hope to hear of this excellent enterprise being completed in a very short time, and then the inhabitants of the Rhondda Valley and Pontypridd will no longer have to submit to the tedious journey of going to Cardiff en route for Newport and the North.—The Clydach Valley from Glyncoch farm to Ynysybwl is alive with the sounds of the "navvies'" implements, and already a road whereon the outcome of the Stephenson's modest invention may be allowed to have its run, has made its appearance, of course the line is most completed, nor are the pits sunk at Ynysybwl yet, but these are things we are earnestly looking forward to, although at the sacrifice of so pretty a valley, that Lord Aberdare was once heard to say, "It is the prettiest I have seen." But commerce and trade override all things, and we hope this will help to stimulate to no considerable degree the wealth and industry of Pontypridd and district.

PONTYPRIDD, CAERPHILLY, AND NEWPORT RAILWAY.

It was hoped that this railway would have been opened for traffic at the commencement of this month. Owing, however, to a defect in one of the abutments of the bridge crossing the River Taff at Pontypridd, men re pulling it down and propping the girders with timber, so that many months must now elapse before the re-construction will be completed.

Top left The line under construction – an extract from the *Pontypridd Chronicle*, 23 April 1881.

Middle left A further report, from the *Pontypridd Observer*, dated 18 June 1881. *Pontypridd Public Library*

Bottom left Last-minute delay - an extract from the *Pontypridd Chronicle* of 26 January 1884. *Pontypridd Public Library*

Right A coal train travels as far as Bassaleg – *Pontypridd Chronicle*, 6 July 1884.

Below The railway is complete, and an arrangement reached with the Taff Vale - an extract from the *Pontypridd Chronicle*, 16 August 1884. *Pontypridd Public Library*

THE PONTYPRIDD CAERPHILLY AND NEWPORT RAILWAY.

The half-yearly meeting of the shareholders of this company was held on Friday, at 60, Gracechurch-street, London, near the chairmanship of Mr C. J. Parkinson, managing director.--The Chairman in moving the adoption of the report said he had great pleasure in informing them that since their last meeting their railway had been completed, and was now in perfect working order, with a double line of rails, capable of carrying any amount of traffic capable of being shipped at Newport. But from causes of a temporary and evanescent character, there has been some annoying obstruction at the Basseleg end of their railway. This had brought out clearly the wisdom of the course adopted last year, when Parliament, in spite of a determined and powerful opposition, granted this company powers for continuing their line direct to the Alexandra Docks, thus giving Newport an independent access to the great coalfields of South Wales. This new portion of their railway and the necessary sidings and adjuncts in connection therewith were in course of construction, and were capable of being completed early in the ensuing year. By these means, and by virtue of an important working agreement with the Taff Vale Railway, which had been entered into for a long period of years, Newport had been made practically part of the Taff Vale Railway system, giving that efficient line an additional port, and providing independent and unfettered access to and from Newport from the Rhondda and all other valleys on the Taff Vale system. This arrangement was of incalculable importance to the colliery owners and freighters, as it would, they believed, place Newport, with its easy and safe access and unrivalled shipping facilities, on as favourable terms for export and import to and from the Rhondda and other valleys as any other port or harbour in the Bristol Channel.—Mr J. S. Adams seconded the motion, which was carried unanimously, and the proceedings closed with a vote of thanks to the chairman.

THE PONTYPRIDD, CAERPHILLY AND NEWPORT RAILWAY.

The first coal train ran along this line on Monday and went without a hitch as far as Beneleg, where it was stopped by one of the Great Western Railway men, acting under instructions, as the agreement for running powers over that line had not been come to.

Below Report on the PC&N/TVR agreement in the *Pontypridd Chronicle*, 28 June 1884. *Pontypridd Public Library*

THE WORKING OF THE PONTYPRIDD AND CAERPHILLY RAILWAY.

AGREEMENT BETWEEN THE TAFF VALE RAILWAY COMPANY AND SIR G. ELLIOT.

On Friday, Sir George Elliot informed the Parliamentary Committee inquiring into the Barry Dock Railway Bill that he and Mr Inskip, the Chairman of the Taff Vale Railway Company had that day signed an agreement by which the Pontypridd, Caerphilly, and Newport line would be worked by the Taff Vale people. He denied that it was an attempt to throw dust into the eyes of the Committee, but a definite arrangement come to, so that the Taff Vale Company would have an alternate route to Cardiff (by means of the Pontypridd Company's running powers over the Rhymney line) and the Rhondda colliery proprietors would have a way to Newport Docks. The following is the text of the agreement:—"Heads of arrangement made the 20th day of June, 1884, between the Taff Vale Railway Company (hereinafter called the Taff company) of the one part, and the Pontypridd, Caerphilly, and Newport Railway Company (hereinafter called the Pontypridd Company). (1) Upon the opening of the Pontypridd Company's railways for such goods and mineral traffic as hereinafter mentioned, the Taff Vale Railway Company with, so far as they lawfully can, having regard to the existing rights of the other companies or persons, provide locomotive power and work from the Pontypridd Junction south of Pontypridd all goods and mineral traffic passing from the Taff Vale Railway to the Pontypridd, Caerphilly, and Newport Railway at Pontypridd Junction, and consigned to and destined for Newport and places beyond; to interchange sidings at or near the junction of the Pontypridd Company's railway and the Alexandra Dock Company's railway, and will also provide locomotive power, and work to Pontypridd Junction all goods and mineral traffic over the Pontypridd Company's railway, and consigned to places on the Taff Company's system, or any intermediate place between the same interchange sidings and Pontypridd. (2) The Taff Vale Company shall not be required to convey from Pontypridd Junction to the said interchange sidings laden trucks of less than 26 wagons or trucks, or to make more than two abunch thereof at the interchange sidings, which shall at all times be kept clear from the reception of such laden traffic. (3) The Taff Vale Company shall convey the return empties from the said sidings in fair average trains, but the return empties shall be properly sorted and placed ready for their several destinations by the Pontypridd Company. (4) The railways over which the Taff Vale Company shall be required to convey traffic in pursuance of these heads of agreement, shall be provided with all necessary sidings, signals, junctions, and other conveniences, and the said railways, signals, sidings, junctions, and other conveniences shall be maintained in good and sufficient working order by the Pontypridd Company, who shall erect and maintain, and keep and supply a sufficient water tank at a convenient place at the interchange sidings, and the Taff Vale Company's engineer shall be supplied with water therefrom free of cost. The Pontypridd Railway Company shall pay and discharge all road tolls, sidings, and other charges payable in respect of any traffic which shall be worked by the Taff Vale Company under this agreement, and shall provide any extra engine power required for taking traffic up the Machen incline. (6) The Taff Comany shall, in respect of coal and coke conveyed by them between the junction at Pontypridd of the Taff Vale Company and the Pontypridd, Caerphilly, and Newport Railway, and the junction east of Caerphilly of the Rhymney Company, and the Brecon and Merthyr Tydvil Junction Railway, and between the Brecon and Merthyr Junction Railway and the Alexandra Dock sidings, be paid by the Pontypridd Company one farthing per ton per mile, and in like proportion for a less distance, and for other goods such sum as in default of agreement shall be from time to time fixed by an arbitrator appointed by the Board of Trade on the application of either party hereto, with the usual clearing-house allowances. The Taff Vale Company shall also in respect of coal and coke traffic conveyed by them between the said junction east of Caerphilly and the said interchange sidings, be paid by the Pontypridd Company 24.100d (twenty-four one-hundredths of a penny) per ton per mile and in like proportion for a less distance, and for other goods, such sum as in default of agreement shall be from time to time fixed by an arbitrator, appointed by the Board of Trade, on the application of either party, with the usual clearing-house allowances. (7) All-through rates for goods carried to the Taff Vale Company's system over the line of the Pontypridd Company shall be subject to the consent of the Taff Vale Company, or an arbitrator under this agreement. (8) Payment to be made monthly by the Pontypridd Company, and that company to settle with other companies. (9) Signalmen, stores, and all costs of sidings and junction expenses at and between Pontypridd Junction and the said interchange sidings to be provided by and at the expense of the Pontypridd Company. (10) Until the completion and opening for traffic of the Pontypridd Company's authorised railway between the Brecon and Merthyr Tydvil Junction Railway and the Alexandra Dock sidings, the Taff Company shall work on the terms before mentioned, the traffic referred to between the said Pontypridd Junction and interchange sidings at Bassaleg to be provided by the Pontypridd Company. (11) Except as herein expressly provided, nothing in this agreement shall affect any of the existing agreements between the companies or any provision in force in favour of the company. (12) Any dispute between the parties hereto not provided for shall be settled in accordance with the provisions of the Railway Companies Arbitration Act, 1859. (13) This agreement to remain in force for ten years from the 1st July, 1884, and to be afterwards subject to six months' notice on either side. (14) A formal agreement embodying the above terms to be settled between the parties by Mr Phipton Beale, or, in failing by some counsel to be named by the Attorney-General, who shall have power to add such other provisions as he shall think expedient for carrying out the intention of the parties hereto as herein expressed. For the Taff Vale Railway Company, James Inskip, chairman. For the Pontypridd, Caerphilly, and Newport Railway, George Elliot."

Pontypridd, Caerphilly and Newport district map of 1910, showing existing railways and proposed deviations. *Courtesy Alan Powell*

The through passenger service started on 28 December 1887 with three trains each way, based at Pontypridd and running from the town's TVR station direct to Newport. This service was worked entirely by the staff of the ANDR until 1 January 1899, when agreement was reached for GWR staff to take over the through services, which in 1892 had increased to four trains each way, worked from Newport.

On 1 September 1904 the ANDR took over the local passenger service, running from its own Pontypridd Tram Road Halt to the Rhymney Railway's Caerphilly station. Following a review, from 1 January 1917, during the First World War period, the service was extended to run into the Brecon & Merthyr's station at Machen, where connections were made with the B&M trains to Newport.

The passenger service usually consisted of a 'push-pull'-fitted engine with one or two coaches, or one of the 'local' service railmotor sets, which had been introduced in September 1904. They were crewed by ANDR staff until 1922, when the line became part of the GWR group.

The ANDR acquired the PC&N by an Act of Parliament of 6 August 1897, but it was not until 31 December that the staff of the ANDR actually took over the general duties on the line. Although the board of directors of the ANDR had instigated the birth of the PC&N for their benefit, for tax and capital investment purposes the PC&N remained a separate railway company.

The PC&N junction was located at the southern end of Pontypridd station, 16 chains from the PC&N's Interchange Sidings West signal box, and officially opened on 7 July 1884 for the handling of mineral traffic, although it had in fact been brought into use by July 1883 for construction purposes in connection with the new line. This photograph, dated 13 July 1958, shows the PC&N line from PCN Junction, facing towards Treforest TVR station; the junction can be seen just past the platform water pump, heading off to the left and crossing the PCN Tramroad bridge in the centre of the photograph. Further left can be seen the PC&N viaduct that crossed the River Taff and carried the line towards Glyntaff. The signal box is PCN Junction. Originally trains from Caerphilly ran into the TVR's Pontypridd station via PCN Junction, but the ANDR was not prepared to pay the TVR's extra charges for the use of the junction or station, so subsequently the services terminated at Tram Road Halt. Because there was no crossover there, the return train had to be propelled for 400 yards 'wrong line' to the crossover at the PCN's Interchange Sidings signal box near Glyntaff Halt, where it could be crossed on to the correct line. This section of the PC&N from PCN Junction to the Glyntaff Interchange Sidings ground frame closed to all traffic on 31 July 1967. *J. J. Davis*

The line today

The PC&N trackbed from Pontypridd Tramroad Halt, which crossed the River Taff before travelling along the embankment that led to the Interchange Sidings at Pentrebach, has all been swept away to become part of the new Pontypridd and Rhondda bypass road. So thorough has this road-building programme been that today, some five years after this inner relief road was started, it is impossible to recognise any of the past scenes of this area.

The cycle track from Rhydyfelin to Penrhos, along the former PC&N trackbed, was initially taken over by the Taff Ely Council, with help from Manpower Services and a community task force, and was renamed the Taff Trail. First a tarmac surface was laid on the part of the trackbed that passes through the Rhydyfelin housing estate, edged with the occasional group of upright posts, like rows of giant dominoes just waiting to be tipped! Upon leaving Rhydyfelin, and heading towards Upper Boat, the trackbed reverts to stone dust and small ballast, bounded by ranch-type fencing now that it has left the built-up area and entered fairly open countryside. This 3½-mile section alone cost £42,000. At Groeswen the path enters the countryside proper, passing beneath an umbrella of branches; the picnic area here reflects the natural peace of the place. At Nantgarw the trackbed is broken by the road to Caerphilly – the former cutting was filled in long ago – and after crossing the road it is only a short distance to Penrhos.

THROUGH TRAINS TO NEWPORT.

Councillor Moses Jones's Suggestion.

At the meeting of the Pontypridd Council on Tuesday (Councillor David Williams presiding)), Councillor Moses Jones outlined his notice of motion: "That representations be made to the railway authorities concerned, urging them to revert to the former custom of running the train service between Pontypridd, Caerphilly and Newport into the Pontypridd T.V.R. station."

Mr. Jones pointed out that to get to Newport and to towns beyond Newport passengers had to go via Cardiff, thus losing a great deal of time. He suggested that the Chairman should see the authorities of the Great Western Railway and the Ministry of Transport to see if the trains could be run through from Pontypridd to Newport. This would also do away with the undesirable sight of people waiing in all weathers for the train at the halt.

It was decided to adopt the recommendation of Councillor Moses Jones.

Left Pontypridd Observer, *5 November 1921*

Right Pontypridd Observer, *30 November 1904*

Below left A closer, and rather picturesque, view of the PC&N junction in 1952, the line branching off the former TVR Cardiff and Merthyr main line and passing over the Broadway, which was formerly known as the Tramroad; the light engine seen here is approximately where the PC&N's Tram Road Halt was located. In the background can be seen the vast area that was known as the Interchange Sidings, while Glyntaff Halt was situated at the base of the cliffs in the distance. The new Pontypridd bypass runs along the former PC&N route from Interchange Sidings to the Broadway. *R. Wilding, courtesy D. J. Rees*

Right Pontypridd Tram Road Halt was opened on 1 September 1904 for local passenger services. It was on that date that the Board of Trade inspected and passed the arrangements made for what was then classed as a 'motor car service' between Pontypridd and Caerphilly. The Board's report stated that the Halt consisted of a ground platform, ie wooden planks placed side by side, very cheap and effective (that is until they got wet and slippery), and that this platform was on the up side only, with both up and down passengers using it. The report also stated that this and the other new platforms were to be provided with a lamp at the entrance barrier of the footpath approaches, and that these barriers were to be opened by the conductors on the arrival of the cars. On 28 April 1906 Lt-Col E. Druitt RE reported to the Board of Trade that he had inspected the new motor car platform, ie the rebuilt Tram Road Halt. He stated that the old car platform at rail level had been replaced by one 100 feet long by 10 feet wide, and 3ft 6ins above rail level, and that the old shelter has been extended, with a ladies' waiting room with conveniences added, and additional lighting provided. The platform was reached by a ramp, well fenced and closed by a gate, and access could only be gained to the platform when a motor car was about to leave. New signalling at the Halt meant that the old arrangement of working wrong line was abolished from 1 May 1906; a new signal box, Interchange Sidings West, was provided at the far end of the river bridge in the Glyntaff direction.

This photograph shows the rebuilt Tram Road Halt, which opened on 1 May 1906, looking towards the TVR's Pontypridd station in June 1921; the Halt was closed

We understand that the new motor coaches of the Newport and Caerphilly Railway will stop to let down and take up passengers near the bridge on the Tramroad. They will thus avoid coming into Pontypridd station and make the Tramroad more of a street for traffic.

entirely by the Great Western Railway Company on 10 July 1922, just over a year later. *D. K. Jones*

Above The PC&N viaduct spanning the River Taff at Pontypridd, situated a few yards from Tram Road Halt, photographed on 29 June 1963. In June 1986 the piers of the viaduct and the site of the former Tram Road Halt were demolished to make a car park. Today the trackbed from Interchange Sidings to the abutments of the PC&N Tram Road bridge, which for many years was left for nature to reclaim, has gone, and now forms part of the new relief road bypassing Pontypridd. *Courtesy J. J. Davis*

Above The firm of Brown, Lenox of Pontypridd, originally known as the Newbridge Anchor & Chain Works, was first awarded Admiralty contracts in 1808. Following the signing of a formal contract between the firm and the PC&N on 14 November 1907, a siding was provided at the works for the transportation of forgings and castings by the PC&N to the ANDR docks at Newport. This photograph circa 1910 shows a general view of the Brown, Lenox Works next to the Glamorgan Canal. The PC&N line was situated at the far end of the works and can be glimpsed going off towards the trees in the top left-hand corner. *Pontypridd Public Library*

Left A Brown, Lenox & Co Ltd advertisement circa 1914. *ANDR booklet of 1914, Newport Harbour Commissioners Office*

BROWN, LENOX & CO., LTD.
Admiralty Contractors for over 100 Years. **Pontypridd and London.**
MANUFACTURERS OF
Chain Cables, Buoys, Moorings & Anchors.

Supply all the principal Harbours and Docks in the World with Buoys and Moorings, and have supplied NEWPORT with all the Buoys and Moorings for the Dock now being opened, and those at present in use.

Above right This photograph taken circa 1906 in the Brown, Lenox Works shows one of the GWR open plank wagons used by the PC&N, in this case one of the four-plank examples of 10 tons tare. The chain links on display here were part of a shipment that was en route to the Cunard Steam Ship Company, bound for their vessel the *Aquitania* then at anchor in the River Mersey. *Messrs Brown, Lenox & Co*

Right An inside view of the works circa 1910. In 1858 Isambard Kingdom Brunel visited here to purchase chains for his ship, the all-metal PSS *Great Eastern*, a steamship that was six times longer than any ship afloat at the time. The well-known photograph of him being 'hung in chains' was taken during that visit. *Messrs Brown, Lenox & Co*

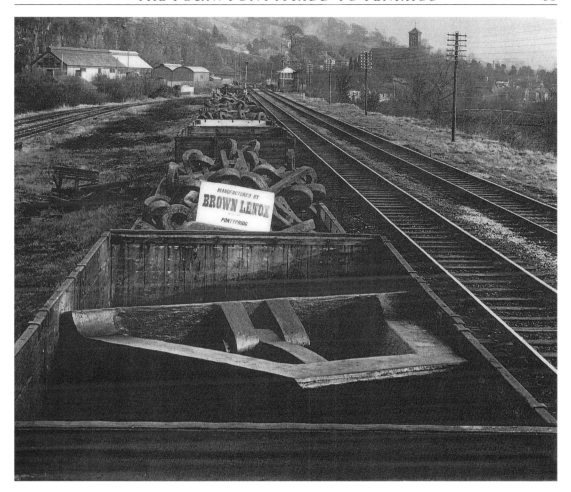

Left Part of an Ordnance Survey map showing the Interchange Sidings (top left), Glyntaff Halt (centre, where the line crosses Pentrebach Road) and Treforest Halt (below right). Interchange Sidings were some 30 chains in length with signal boxes situated at the east and west ends, and were used for the marshalling and interchange of all types of traffic. By 1904 there was also a considerable amount of general trade being handled at the PC&N goods station at Glyntaff en route to and from the Alexandra Docks. However, in the GWR summer timetable of 1938 there was a paragraph that stated that the signal box was to be opened only as required, thus showing that trade had dropped quite a lot by then.

On 2 January 1967 the PC&N line from Interchange Sidings to Penrhos Junction, which by then was operated by a hand-operated ground frame located at the Interchange Sidings end, was closed and locked out of use permanently. *Reproduced from the 1943 Ordnance Survey map*

Above Including a wealth of detail, this photograph shows the Interchange Sidings East signal box shortly after its closure. Opposite the box is the former carriage shed, and on the left the Quarry Sidings, while the Brown, Lenox wagons, on their own siding, are carrying mooring chains rather than the anchor chains that were the common traffic from the

factory. The houses to the right of the box are known as Nightingales Bush, past which runs the Glamorganshire Canal. Above the houses is St Mary's Church, and the footbridge on the extreme fight crosses the River Taff. By the lack of leaves on the trees, the photograph was probably taken in February 1962. *Alun Powell collection*

Below An extract from the *Pontypridd Chronicle* of 6 August 1881. *Pontypridd Public Library*

GLYNTAF.

THE NEW RAILWAY BRIDGE.—The bridge erected on the road to Craig-yr-Haulfa village, over the Pontypridd and Caerphilly Railway, is, it appears at present, likely to result in an action at law being instituted by the owners of property in that village against the company, their plea being that the ascent to the bridge is so steep, without, as they allege, the slightest reason for it, as to make the village difficult of access, and thereby seriously depreciates the value of the houses in the locality. The ascent is so steep that vehicular traffic is almost impossible, and hauliers already decline to take fuel in carts to the scores of houses above the bridge.

Above left Glyntaff was opened on 1 September 1904. Later, after the Grouping, it was renamed Glyntaff Halt by the GWR on 1 July 1924. It closed to passenger services on 5 May 1932. This postcard view circa 1910 shows the Halt on the extreme left, while in the centre foreground is the goods shed and railway bridge over the Pentrebach Road. The railway bridge in the extreme right-hand corner takes the line over the Glamorganshire Canal (see the map on page 82). In 1906 the Glyntaff goods station's telephone number was '31 National', a far cry from the length of today's numbers! The postcard is captioned 'Treforest', which is the area beyond the halt; it was a locally issued card that was on sale in many of the shops in the town at that time.

Unfortunately the southern end of the site is out of sight. It was there that the engine shed was located, opened on 1 September 1904 and equipped with full engine facilities; it closed in September 1922. The railmotor shed on the up side was provided in 1906 and removed in 1930, although the siding was not removed until 2 February 1947. In the ANDR Appendix of May 1906 instructions regarding the 'motor car services' stated that payments must be made to the Glyntaff agent.

One siding in the goods yard was extended to handle the traffic from the Pentrebach Quarry under an agreement of 26 February 1903 with J. Gibb. By 20 June 1925 the quarry was being worked by the Albion Coal Company, and the former agreement was terminated.

Today all traces of the Halt have been erased by the A470 trunk road, which now covers the site. The goods depot has also gone and the site where it stood is now part of a warehouse and storage building. The shed area is now in a neglected state, overgrown and covered with brambles. Even the cutting that carried the line past St Mary's Church is impossible to follow due to being densely wooded. *Pontypridd Public Library*

Left Another slightly broader postcard view of Treforest village, circa 1910. In the foreground is again Glyntaff Halt, and on the right-hand side part of the goods shed. In the middle can be seen the goods siding and the Halt's waiting room. On the left is the Glamorganshire Canal, passing by Pontypridd Gasworks in the top left-hand corner; the gasworks also had a contract with the PC&N. The river is the River Taff.

The coaches in the foreground are the former Barnum & Bailey circus coaches. Also in view is one of the former Mersey Railway coaches, a four-wheeler Brake 3rd, which was purchased in September 1904.

In the Board of Trade recommendations of 1904 the Halt was to be of the ground platform type, but as can clearly be seen in this postcard it now has a raised platform. It is possible that this was done on 28 April 1906 when Tram Road Halt was similarly rebuilt. *Author's collection*

Above ANDR engine No 14, formerly GWR No 1426, with driver Owen Morgan and fireman Garnet Lang in a photograph taken circa 1919 at Glyntaff after she had a received a new boiler at Hawthorn Leslie's works in December 1919. This '517' Class engine was one of two permanently shedded at Glyntaff shed. *Welsh Industrial & Maritime Museum, Cardiff*

Below A map showing Pontypridd Gasworks and Sidings. On 10 December 1896 an agreement was signed with the ANDR for the construction of a siding to transport coal to the gasworks, which was in the control of the Pontypridd Urban District Council. A further agreement was signed with the GWR on 16 September 1926 for closure of the signal box, which was replaced by a ground frame to work the sidings; the crossover was removed at the same time. The sidings were listed in the 1904 edition of the *Railway Clearing House Hand-book of Stations* under the ANDR, but it is presumed that they were serviced by the TVR until 1906.

A Board of Trade report of 9 April 1908 concerning the sidings stated: 'I have inspected the new sidings at Gasworks Sidings, further interlocking is required and that the signal box there contains 13 working and one spare lever.' A ground frame, worked by the guards on the goods trains, was installed in 1931 for the working of the sidings on the up side of the line; these sidings were situated 588 yards from Interchange East signal box. The private siding agreement was terminated on 29 September 1953 and both sidings and the ground frame were taken out of use on 23 May 1954.

Today no trace is left of Gasworks Sidings. Even the impressive dressed stone building was demolished in October 1990, and a car park now covers the whole area. *Reproduced from the 1943 Ordnance Survey map*

Below ANDR engine No 21 hauling logs on a Treforest to Caerphilly goods train, photographed near Treforest at the Gasworks Sidings. This 0-6-0 saddle tank engine was built by Messrs R. Stephenson, and renumbered by the GWR as 670. Photographed on 19 May 1919, it was withdrawn from service in 1926. *LCGB (Ken Nunn Collection)*

Map showing the line from Glyntaff (top left-hand corner) to Dynea via Rhydyfelin. *Reproduced from the 1938 Ordnance Survey map*

Below An extract from the *Pontypridd Chronicle* of 25 June 1881. *Pontypridd Public Library*

Bottom Treforest Halt on 9 June 1952, looking towards Rhydyfelin. Situated in a cutting with an overbridge next to it, Treforest opened on 1 September 1904 for local passenger services; it was renamed by the GWR as Treforest Halt on 1 July 1924. The shelters seen here are typical of the GWR's policy on spending money on this line, and one can see that no expense was spared! The sign beyond the fence reads 'GWR. Trespassers will be prosecuted'. The Halt closed on 17 September 1956, and today the site is covered by the extended playing field of the nearby comprehensive school. *The late Mr T. B. Sands, courtesy of Westrail Enterprises*

Opposite above Rhydyfelin PC&N Halt was another of the stations opened on 1 September 1904 for local passenger services. The company even provided an occupational crossing for travellers to reach the down platform. Situated 1½ miles from Pontypridd, the station was renamed by the GWR in 1922 as Rhydyfelin High Level Halt, so as not to be confused with the nearby Halt of the former Cardiff

Railway. According to *Clinker's Register* the Halt closed on 14 May 1928.

The Halt consisted of a sleeper-type wooden platform at ground level, and is seen here in June 1921 looking towards Dynea. A GWR locomotive is pulling a Barnum & Bailey coach and a converted railmotor trailer; the engine was on loan to the PC&N because the company's regular engine, No 14, was out of service. On the left can be seen one of the numerous cast iron notices, this one reading 'Beware of trains running in both directions when crossing'. *D. K. Jones*

Opposite below This second Rhydyfelin Halt was opened by the GWR on 14 May 1928, 18 chains to the east of the PC&N facility; the Halt was thus a distance of 8m 79ch from Machen Junction. It was this halt that was the cause of the destruction of autotrailer steps on forgetful occasions. It was the responsibility of the guard to ensure that the steps were raised or lowered on the approach to or when the leaving the halts along the line, but sometimes it was easier to leave them in place, especially as all of the PC&N halts were at ground level; however, this GWR-built halt was a raised platform type, and if the guard was new or forgetful the effect was dramatic, much to the amusement of his colleagues!

This photograph, taken on 27 August 1948, shows a passenger train on the Pontypridd to Caerphilly service pulled by former GWR 0-6-0PT No 6438; the leading trailer is of Rhymney Railway origin. It is interesting to note that while the platform seen on the left was of wooden construction, the other was of concrete. Note also the GWR corrugated tin shelter, which was typical of the type of shelter provided for the company's customers at these lower-classified halts. Rhydyfelin Halt closed on 8 June 1953, and today no trace can be seen of either station; the grey scar of the trackbed is now part of the Treforest to Nantgarw cycle track. *I. L. Wright*

TREFOREST.

A MAN IN THE CANAL.—One of the "navvies" engaged on the Pontypridd and Caerphilly Railway here, had a narrow escape from drowning in the canal the other night, he was rescued by the proprietor of the Llanbradach Arms, who brought him to the bank by the hair of his head, owing to the darkness of the night the poor fellow must have missed his footing. There is a great public danger still existing along the Pentrebach road, in the form of unprotected openings in the wall bounding the canal.

Above Dynea was opened on 1 September 1904, and this photograph, taken in October 1908, shows the damage that resulted from heavy rain swelling the small stream above the halt and causing an avalanche of water and stones to flood the area, before overspilling into the nearby Glamorganshire Canal and causing a great deal more damage. The Halt can be seen up the path on the left, with workmen from the local authority clearing away the flood damage from the road running under the railway. Dynea was renamed by the GWR as Dynea Halt on 1 July 1924. Today no evidence of the Halt remains; like most of the facilities along this line, the buildings and wooden fencing have long gone, and even the soil that lay under the ballast has been removed to form a slipway from the track level to the base of the bridge foundations to form part of the new cycle track. *Courtesy of Starling Press*

Below This photograph shows Dynea Halt on 14 July 1956 looking somewhat the worse for wear just two months before

closure, looking towards Upper Boat. A down siding, which was controlled by Dynea signal box, was located some 300 yards towards Upper Boat Halt, giving access to Dynea Colliery. This was added by the GWR in 1931, and at some later date a ground frame was installed, operated by the train guard. However, this siding must have been short-lived, as by 1943 the Ordnance Survey map shows no evidence of it. *R. M. Casserley*

Right This map shows just how close the various railway lines were, and the competition for mineral and passenger traffic was a real battle before the GWR did some pruning. Upper Boat, in the top left-hand corner, again opened on 1 September 1904 for local passenger services. The Board of Trade report stated that a foot overbridge had been provided to save passengers crossing the line to reach the down-side platform. It was renamed Upper Boat Halt by the GWR on 1 July 1924, and the GWR timetable for that year and again in 1926 shows it as a request stop only, and then only on certain passenger trains; it had not taken the GWR long to begin cutting back on parts of its newly acquired services. Upper Boat closed entirely to both goods and passenger services on 17 September 1956. Groeswen Halt can be seen in the centre of the map, and Nantgarw at the bottom. *Reproduced from the 1921 Ordnance Survey map*

Above Groeswen station opened for local passenger services on 1 September 1904. After the Grouping, as with the other halts along this line, it was renamed by the GWR on 1 July 1924 as Groeswen Halt. This 1904 photograph looking towards Dynea shows the Halt, footpath and signal box all in a very tidy and clean state; it was possibly taken by the company photographer shortly after its opening to the public. Note the unusual arrangement of the colliery siding connection passing through the ground-level down 'platform'. The house above the Halt at the end of the road bridge was the manager's house-cum-weighbridge for the tramroad leading from Groeswen Colliery to the siding at the Halt. Groeswen was perhaps unusual as the ground-level down line platform had the siding connection running through it, as can be seen. This line was added in 1899 to connect with the colliery sidings, which already existed. A down refuge siding was added in 1907, and taken out of use on 21 January 1949, although the crossover remained until 28 September 1952. *Pontypridd Public Library*

Below The site of Groeswen Halt seen from track level under the road bridge and looking in the opposite direction on 10 July 1958. The Halt had closed on 17 September 1956, and Groeswen Siding signal box (2m 63ch from Interchange Sidings East) was demolished in the same year, but the water crane as well as the somewhat dilapidated fencing survive. In 1988 the trackbed was cleared and is also now part of the new cycle track, with a picnic area on the site of the Halt. The stone retaining wall behind the signal box remains, and is the only indication of where the Halt stood. *R. M. Casserley*

Above ANDR engine No 14 photographed at speed with the 10.20am Pontypridd to Caerphilly train, photographed near Nantgarw on 19 May 1919. *LCGB (Ken Nunn Collection)*

Below Nantgarw Halt was another of the stations opened for local passenger services on 1 September 1904, and was renamed Nantgarw High Level by the GWR on 1 July 1924; it closed entirely on 17 September 1956. This photograph, looking towards Groeswen on 4 September 1956, shows former GWR 0-6-0PT No 6411 arriving at the Halt with the 2.52pm Pontypridd to Machen auto-train.

Today it is only by the use of old and new Ordnance Survey maps that it is possible to pinpoint the locations of these former halts. Most of them, including those at Groeswen and Nantgarw, were situated next to road bridges; these, some no wider than a horse and cart, are a good guide to their location. *S. Rickard*

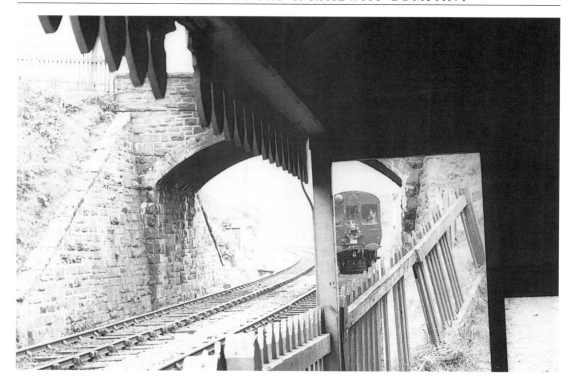

Above Another photograph of the auto-train service, now being propelled by No 6411, as it approaches Nantgarw Halt on its return journey to Pontypridd on 15 September 1956. This was rather a sad day, not only for the nearby residents that used this service, but also for railway enthusiasts, as it was the last day of the service between Pontypridd and Newport via Caerphilly before the final closure.

On 22 October 1987 the *Pontypridd Observer* reported that plans were to go ahead to convert part of the former PC&N line from Glyntaff Cemetery to Nantgarw Road into part of the Taff Valley Cycleway, and credit must be given to the Taff Ely Council and the local Community Project members for making use of this former line, which over the years was beginning to revert to nature. *S. C. L. Phillips and D. K. Jones*

Left The ANDR announcement of the 'Motor Car' Sunday service, *Pontypridd Observer*, 4 June 1911. *Pontypridd Public Library*

NOTICE.

Alexandra (Newport & South Wales) Docks and Railway Company.

MOTOR CAR SERVICE

Commencing on JUNE 4th, 1911, a

SUNDAY SERVICE

Will be Run between

Pontypridd and Caerphilly

Calling at Intermediate Stations.

The Sunday Service will be provisional and experimental, and the Company do not bind themselves to the continuance thereof.

Full particulars of times and trains, see Company's Time Tables.

JOHN MACAULAY,

Newport, Mon., May, 1911.   General Manager.

Right Extracts from the Taff Vale Railway Company Rule Book of 1894, regarding working on the PC&N line. *Courtesy Mr D. G. Thomas*

When descending the main and other severe inclines the Driver must give 1 crow to stop putting Brakes down and 2 crows to lift Brakes when too many are applied.

SPECIAL INSTRUCTIONS TO ENGINEMEN AND SIGNALMEN.

UP TRAINS.—Up Rhondda Trains, having no work to do short of Pontypridd Junction, when approaching Treforest North must give **one crow.** The signalman must give **1-2** on the bell for the line upon which the train is travelling to P. C. and N. Junction immediately after sending "Train on Line," so that when P. C. and N. Junction asks **"Is line clear"** of Pontypridd Junction he may use the **"Is line clear for Branch Goods"** code.

Up Trains having work to do at Pontypridd Station, New Warehouse, or Pontshon Norton, or requiring to stop at Pontypridd for Water, must give three short whistles twice, thus /// pause /// when approaching Treforest North, and the signalmen there must, immediately after sending "Train on Line," give **1-2-1** on the Bell for the line on which the Train is travelling to P. C. and N. Junction, where the train will be dealt with as may be expedient.

DOWN TRAINS.—The following engine whistles must be given at :—

Gyfeillon Lower, if they have no work to do at Coke Ovens.

Rhondda Cutting Junction, after completing work at Coke Ovens.

Pontshon Norton, if they have no work to do at Pontypridd Warehouse.

Pontypridd Northern, after completing work at Pontypridd Warehouse.

By Trains proceeding to P. C. and N.—**3 long and 1 crow.**

By Trains proceeding to No. 2—**2 long.**

The signalman at the respective cabins, on hearing the whistles named, must immediately after sending "Train on Line," send the bell signals (shown on page 23) to the signal cabin in advance, and when sent from Gyfeillon Lower or Pontshon Norton, must be transmitted to Pontypridd Junction to enable Pontypridd Junction (for Trains going to P. C. and N., when asking **"Is Line Clear"** of P. C. and N. Junction) to use the Code **"Is Line Clear for Branch Goods"**; or (for Trains going to No. 2 Down Road, after asking P. C. and N. Junction "Is Line Clear for Ordinary Goods or Mineral Train") to send the specified Bell Code forward.

23

The Bell Codes are :—

Trains to P. C. and N.	**1-2.**
„ No. 2 Down	**1-2-1.**

The Drivers of through Trains proceeding to any Branch on approaching the Signal Cabin next but one before reaching the Junction, must sound the standard whistle according to the Line they are on, and the Signalman must immediately after sending "Train on Line" give **3-5** to the Signal Cabin in advance, to enable the Signal Cabin in the rear of the Junction to ask **"Is Line Clear for Branch Goods"** of the Junction Signal Cabin.

The Driver of a through Train that may require to pass from one road to another through a facing shunt, must at the second Signal Cabin next but one to that having control of the shunt (or the next one to it, if circumstances such as having to do work at intermediate Sidings should render it necessary), sound the standard whistle according to the Line on which he is running, and the Signalman on hearing it must immediately after sending "Train on Line" give the following Codes on the Bell for the Line on which the Train is travelling, to the Signal Cabin in advance :—

From No. 1 to No. 2 Road	**2-5**
„ No. 2 „ 1 „	**5-2**

to enable the Signalman where the change is required to be made, to ask and obtain "Line Clear" from the Signal Cabin in advance for the Line upon which the Train requires to proceed.

SPECIAL WHISTLES.   Main Lines (Con.)

STATIONS AND JUNCTIONS.	TO AND FROM	WHISTLES.	REMARKS.
P. C. & N. Junction ...	Old Warehouse Siding...	4 short	
Pontypridd Junction ...	Rhondda Branch	3	
	Chapel Siding	1 crow	
	Down Branch and Bay...	2	
	Up „ „	2 and 1 short	
	Penrhiew Siding	1 crow and 1 short	
	Down Main and Down Branch ...	4 short	
	Crawshay's Sidings and Bay	1 crow and 2 short	

5. THE RHYMNEY AND BRECON & MERTHYR: PENRHOS TO NEWPORT VIA CAERPHILLY

Penrhos Junction was the end of the PC&N line as such, and marked the start of the second phase of the journey, by running alongside the metals of the Rhymney Railway at first, then eventually joining them at Penrhos South Junction to head towards Caerphilly station via the level crossing at Watford Road and Caerphilly West Junction, a distance of some 5m 14ch.

At this point mention of the complex arrangements needed to secure the PC&N's access to Alexandra Docks must be made. As mentioned earlier, on 8 August 1878 Parliament granted that the PC&N could run between a junction with the TVR at Pontypridd to a junction with the Rhymney Railway at Penrhos. By means of running powers granted to the PC&N it could then run over the B&M Caerphilly branch to Bassaleg, where it would join the former Monmouth Railway & Canal Company, by now under the ownership of the GWR, and it was hoped that these powers would be sufficient to gain access to the ANDR lines at West Mendelgief Junction, Newport.

The Taff Vale Railway contracted to work the trains over the PC&N route to Newport Docks in the hope that this would lead to the PC&N becoming part of the TVR system. The first train of coal left Pontypridd on 7 July 1884, calling at Caerphilly station to pick up a Brecon & Merthyr pilot engine. However, on arrival at Bassaleg Junction the GWR declined to allow the PC&N train to pass over the junction.

After a couple of weeks of negotiations, the GWR gave way and the trains began to run into the Alexandra Docks in earnest on 25 July. Needless to say neither the Alexandra Docks nor the PC&N became part of the Taff Vale Railway.

By the Machen Loop Act of 1887 the PC&N was authorised to double the Brecon & Merthyr's Caerphilly branch, and a new down line was laid on a diverging route from Gwaun-y-Bara Junction to Machen, with the former single line becoming the up line; this gave an easier gradient of 1 in 200 for loaded coal trains to climb, rather than the 1 in 39 that they had to face previously. This new up line was brought into use on 14 September 1891, and was then transferred to Brecon & Merthyr ownership. In return the B&M paid 50 per cent of the annual net earnings from its Caerphilly branch to the PC&N.

The line today

The trackbed of the former Rhymney Railway line from Penrhos to Caerphilly now has a tarmac surface and is fenced in places; mostly it is lined with trees and bushes growing along the cutting on either side, with a modern concrete gully that carries the almost constant stream of rainwater that drains from the cutting, helping to reduce the risk of flooding of the trackbed and making the surface slippery for cyclists. At the former Penrhos Junction the piers that supported the former Barry Railway line can be seen, but now gorse bushes and Buddleia dominate the scene. Here there is wildlife in abundance, but not even cyclists will disturb the scene for here the cycle track turns away to follow other routes into Caerphilly. A few hundred yards further on the trackbed ceases, because what was once the Caerphilly branch junction is now filled in and a newly built housing estate has appeared. However, once the estate has been left behind the trackbed returns again on the approach to the former Watford Junction. The short distance from here to Caerphilly has not changed much since my last visit in 1996, and Caerphilly station is also unchanged – not even a pot of paint has been opened, or so it seems!

On the Brecon & Merthyr Railway line, the site of Caerphilly East Junction has also hardly changed since 1996; a little more derelict than before, only the occasional patch of ballast can still be seen among the weeds and grass that grow in abundance here today. Although the former Caerphilly Railway engine shed can still be seen, it is now in private use; all of this area has become an industrial site. The trackbed that crossed over Van Road on its way eastwards towards Gwern-y-Domen, so easy to follow six years before, is now difficult to find. At Gwern-y-Domen Halt there were perhaps more trees and bushes than before, while the site of Gwaun-y-Bara Junction was out of bounds due to the foot and mouth crisis of 2001, but nothing seemed to have changed.

The site of Fountain Bridge Halt was fairly inaccessible in 1996; trees were numerous and it was only the position of the road bridge that gave a clue to the Halt's actual location, from where it was only a short, albeit difficult, walk to see the piers that once held the river bridge. Today it is even worse! Waterloo Halt is still part of someone's garden, and at White Hart the bushes and wild rose brambles have grown more prolific. Machen station, a dirty and derelict building with a burnt-out car abandoned on the platform when seen in 1996, is no more; instead there is now a very impressive house, complete with an extension that covers most of the former trackbed. Only the road bridge, situated alongside this former site, provides an opportunity for comparison.

Machen Quarry, now part of the Lord Hanson Aggregates group, and a part of the ARC Company, produces between 10,000 and 13,000 tons of medium-sized rail ballast a month, which is loaded into PSV railway wagons that are then hauled to the Alexandra Dock Sidings, where they are stabled before transportation to places like Fishguard and Gloucester.

Three years ago Church Road station was bought from the previous owners, and is now undergoing a major renovation; unlike Machen, one can still recognise this building. Outwardly impressive with a combination of old and new, the station approach is now a drive of white gravel chippings, complementing a fine garden and carp pond, while still in place is the platform, its edging of dressed stone sharply reminding visitors of the site's former role. Inside Mr and Mrs Jenkins have made this spacious building attractive, using Mr Jenkins's skills as a retired painter and decorator. It was here that Lord Tredegar had his own private and very grand waiting room, and this has also been given that special Jenkins touch!

At Rhiwderin station, also in private hands, the most recent addition is the white palisade fencing that has replaced the Leylandii trees; even the double garage addition to the side of this former station blends in well.

Bassaleg station is now home to the Junction 28 restaurant, a rather splendid building on the site of what was once a rather secluded station; it is named after the nearby Tredegar Park motorway junction. Various cast iron signs hang on its white pebble-dashed walls, and it has a good reputation for fine food; perhaps it holds a greater attraction for today's visitors than was ever the case in its railway days!

Church Road station on 27 July 2001. Sitting at the picnic table next to the carp pond is Mrs Jenkins senior, talking to the author's friend Alun Powell. The garden is a treat to enjoy on this warm July day! Below the gable end of the station building Lord Tredegar had his own private waiting room. *Author*

Above A map showing Penrhos Junction. In the bottom left-hand corner the PC&N, Rhymney and Barry lines head off to Pontypridd, Taffs Well and Barry respectively. *Reproduced from the 1921 Ordnance Survey map*

Above right The junction at Penrhos was governed by Penrhos North Junction signal box; this was responsible for directing traffic not only for the PC&N and Rhymney Railway, but also the Barry Railway. This rather detailed photograph, looking west on 6 September 1956, shows Penrhos North Junction signal box, of GWR design. The train that can be seen in the distance on the right is the auto-train set for Pontypridd being propelled by engine No 6411 along the PC&N line. On the left is a goods train on the spur

built by the Barry Railway to provide a link between the Rhymney Railway line (the centre pair of tracks) and the Barry Railway, which once crossed the junction on the viaduct the remains of which can be seen. Today the Rhymney line down the 'big bank' is part of a cycle track network stretching from Taffs Well to Caerphilly. *S. C. L. Phillips and D. K. Jones*

Right Photographed from Penrhos Junction signal box on 6 September 1956, an auto-train trailer pulled by a former GWR pannier tank passes under the stone-built overbridge en route to Caerphilly, via the line that can be seen branching off to the right in the distance. *S. C. L. Phillips and D. K. Jones*

Top The section of the Rhymney Railway's line through Caerphilly to Machen was opened in 1867. For a short period the PC&N had its own platform at Caerphilly, shown in this old and rather faded photograph dating from about 1900, before the reconstruction of the station in 1914. This platform was situated on the Penrhos Junction side of the Caerphilly Road bridge, below St Martins Church, passengers obtaining their tickets from the Caerphilly station booking office. Photographed in winter time, the snow gives a clear edge to the path leading from the road to the platform. The remainder of the Rhymney Railway station can be seen under the road bridge.

From 1 April 1908 all PC&N traffic over Rhymney metals was operated with the assistance of Rhymney staff, then on 1 January 1917 the service between Caerphilly and Machen was extended to connect with the Brecon & Merthyr Railway's trains that ran to and from Newport station by using the Rhymney Railway's Senghenydd branch railmotor; this service lasted for a short period only, ceasing on 5 May 1919.

Today the Brecon & Merthyr Railway junction, formerly known as Caerphilly East Junction, can still be seen, a single track of rotted sleepers with their GWR-marked chairs still in position. This track winds its way for a short distance towards Machen; now overgrown with small bushes and weeds, it is another sharp reminder of better days now long gone. *Caerphilly Library*

Middle This view of Caerphilly station was taken from the passenger overbridge, facing east, and shows once again pannier tank No 6411, returning from Newport with its auto-trailer leading, as it approaches the station platforms on 14 September 1956. *S. C. L. Phillips and D. K. Jones*

Bottom Gwern-y-Domen Halt, east of Caerphilly on the Brecon & Merthyr Railway was opened for passenger services in October 1908, and closed entirely on 17 September 1956. Seen here are the rather neglected remains of the Halt on 4 October 1957. By 1996 all traces had vanished, with only a cleared area of trees and the roadbridge abutments marking the spot where the Halt stood and where the line passed as it made its way towards Gwaun-y-Bara Junction. *S. C. L. Phillips and D. K. Jones*

Fountain Bridge Halt was located on the PC&N's Machen Loop line and was served by up trains only. Opening for passenger services in October 1908, it also closed entirely on 17 September 1956. This photograph, taken from the road above this halt on 30 August 1956, gives a clear view of the Halt and the 63-yard viaduct over the river, and shows a former GWR engine of the '51' Class, No 4130, pulling a Caerphilly to Newport train. Today this line is also very overgrown, the trackbed under the road bridge has become waterlogged, and the river bridge has long since been dismantled. *S. C. L. Phillips and D. K. Jones*

Waterloo Halt also opened in October 1908. Being situated on the original Brecon & Merthyr Machen Loop line, it was served by down trains only. This clear photograph, taken on 17 September 1950, gives a good view of the former GWR auto-trailer. The Halt closed with the others on 17 September 1956, and today the site is the garden of a bungalow; the embankment that carried the line can still be followed, but with difficulty. *V. C. Hardacre*

Former GWR '37' Class engine No 3714, built in 1936, is seen here with an auto-trailer approaching Waterloo Halt on 15 September 1956, two days before closure. These three halts originally had timber platforms and were converted to the low ballast type, with movable steps on the auto-coaches, in 1929. *S. C. L. Phillips and D. K. Jones*

Above A former GWR pannier tank with the 4.58pm Machen to Pontypridd auto-train approaches White Hart Halt on 29 August 1956. Opened for passenger services on 12 May 1947, the Halt was located on both the up and down sections of the PC&N Machen Loop line. Today the Halt is long gone, and the embankment that carried the line is now overgrown with brambles and wild roses, effectively hiding all traces. *S. C. L. Phillips and D. K. Jones*

Left A sketch of White Hart Halt showing pannier tank No 6411 waiting for passengers for the last time on the day of closure, 30 June 1952. No 6411 was one of the '64' Class engines, built at Swindon Works in 1934. *The late Mr A. Merchant*

Left An extract from Bradshaw for July 1944 showing the service from Pontypridd to Machen and listing the Halts. The column headed 'A' shows the times of the GWR through service. *Courtesy of T. D. Chapman*

PONTYPRIDD and MACHEN—(Third class only).

Miles	Down		mrn	mrn	mrn	mrn A	mrn B		aft	aft aft S	aft	aft S	aft S		Suns.	
	Pontypridd ¶ ...... dep	7 40	..	8 44	..	9 48	1112	..	2 52	..	4 58 6 17	..	..	8 25 9 23	..	.. ..
	Caerphilly ¶ ...... { arr	8 0	..	9 4	..	10 1	1132	..	3 12	..	5 15 6 37	..	..	8 45 9 43	..	.. ..
	88, 92 ...... { dep	..	..	9 12	..	10 3	1135	..	5 16	..	5 22 ..	..	..	.. 9 45	..	.. ..
6¼	Machen 77 ...... arr	..	..	9 23	..	1011	1146	..	3 25	..	5 33 ..	7 19	..	.. 9 57	..	.. ..

Miles	Up		mrn Z	mrn		mrn	mrn A	aft B		aft	aft aft S	aft	aft S	aft S		Suns.	
	Machen ¶ ...... dep	6 55	..	858 9 26	..	1239	..	3 42	..	536 7 18	..	..	.. 10 5	..	.. ..	
	Caerphilly ¶ ...... { arr	7 5	..	9 69 40	..	1251	..	3 54	..	548 7 29	..	..	.. 1015	..	.. ..	
	88, 92 ...... { dep	..	8 13	9 8 9 41	..	1253	..	4 6	..	549 ..	785	857	.. 1017	..	.. ..	
10¼	Pontypridd ...... arr	..	8 33	922 10 1	..	1 18	..	428	..	6 9 ..	755	917	.. 1037	..	.. ..	

A Not calling at the Halts. Runs to and from Newport, page 77.   B To and from Newport, page 77.
S Sats. only.   Z Workmen's Train to and from Newport, page 77.   Not calling at the Halts.

¶ "Halts" at Treforest, at Rhydfelin (High Level), at Dynes, at Upper Boat, at Groeswen, and at Nantgarw (High Level), between Pontypridd and Caerphilly; at Gwernydomen, at Fountain Bridge, and at Waterloo, between Caerphilly and Machen.

Right Extracts from the Taff Vale Railway Rule Book of 1894 showing special arrangements for operating PC&N trains over the B&M. *Courtesy D. G. Thomas*

SPECIAL WHISTLES.

Main Lines (Con.)

STATIONS AND JUNCTIONS.	TO AND FROM	WHISTLES.	REMARKS.
Llantrisant Junction ...	Siding and No. 2 Up	1 crow and 2	
	Tin Works and No. 1 Down ...	1 crow	
	South Sidings and Branch	1 crow	
Treforest Barry	Forest Steel and No. 2 Up ...	1 crow and 2 short	See Special Instructions, pages 22 and 23.
	Warehouse and No. 1 Down ...	1 crow and 1 short	
	Barry Up and Down and vice versa ...	4 short	
	Barry Up Line Sidings...	1 crow	
Treforest North	Forest Steel Works Siding ...	4 short	
P. C. & N. Railway			See Appendix.
P. C. & N. Junction ...	Main Lines	3 and 1 crow	
	Bay Road and Branch	1 crow and 1 short	Down Main Line Trains will use the Standard Whistle for the road upon which they require to travel
35	,, and Down Line	1 crow and 2 short	

A tail lamp and swing iron must be kept at P.C. and N. Junction to be used by engines returning from Newport, and having to run light on No. 2 Down road to Treforest Barry for empties.

P. C. & N. and B. & M. RAILWAYS.

STATIONS AND JUNCTIONS.	TO AND FROM	WHISTLES.	REMARKS.
Interchange Siding ..	Up and Down Main Line	1	T.V.R. trains will carry 1 White at Chimney, 1 White on left Buffer from Pontypridd to Alexandra Dock.
	Up to Down and vice versa	1 and 2 short	
	Down Main and Full Siding nearest Main Line	1 and 1 short	
	Down Main and No. 2 Full Siding ...	2 short and 1	
	Up Main and Empty Sidings No. 1 ...	2 short	
	,, and ,, No. 2 ...	2 and 2 short	
Quarry Siding	Main Line and Quarry	1 crow	
Penrhos Junction ..	Up and Down	2	
Caerphilly West ...	Up and Down	2	
Caerphilly East ...	Up and Down·	2	
Machen Junction ...	Up and Down	2	Up and Down Main Lines 1 long.
75	Station Sidings	2 short and 1 crow.	

P. C. & N. and B. & M. RAILWAYS (Con.)

STATIONS AND JUNCTIONS.	TO AND FROM	WHISTLES.	REMARKS.
Machen Junction ...	Main Line	1	
	Caerphilly Branch	2	
	Station Sidings	2 short and 1 crow	
	South Sidings	2 short and 1 long	
	North Sidings	3 short	
	Cross over Road	2 crows	
Machen Shop Box ...	Main Line	1	
	Sidings West of Up Line	2 short	
	Locomotive Sidings West of Up Line .	1 short and 1 crow	
	Compound Crossing Up to Down ...	3 short and 1 crow	
Machen Lime Kiln ...	Main Line	1	
	Coal Siding High Level	2	
	Lime Siding Low Level	3	
76	Cross over Road	3 crows	

Below An extract from the *Cardiff Times* of 3 January 1925. *Cardiff Public Library*

Train in Landslide.

FIVE WAGONS WRECKED NEAR MACHEN.

A train of empty wagons was travelling to the Rhondda Valley from Newport on Tuesday night, and when about 1½ miles from Machen Station a landslide was responsible for wrecking five of the wagons.

Fortunately the driver and fireman were able to maintain their posts, and bring the rest of the train to a standstill.

This did not interfere with any of the passenger trains to any great extent, as all the traffic was worked over one road.

Above This view of the Machen loop lines on 14 September 1956 gives a good indication of the steepness of the original line (on the left) and the lesser gradient of the new PC&N line. Approaching on the latter is former GWR '94' Class pannier tank No 8493, built in 1952 by Robert Stephenson & Hawthorns, with the 12.55pm Caerphilly to Newport train. The line on the right is the former Brecon & Merthyr line to Machen via Trethomas. *S. C. L. Phillips and D. K. Jones*

Below This photograph, looking towards the junctions in the last year of the private pre-Grouping companies, June 1921, shows the B&M's Machen station with the PC&N service in the sidings. On the left is the goods shed. Today the trackbed is sadly overgrown with gorse bushes, and small saplings grow unchecked on both the up and down loop lines that came together here; the junction is now fenced off and privately owned. *D. K. Jones*

A more elevated view of Machen station on 21 May 1955, again looking north-west towards Machen Junction. Pannier tank No 6411 is seen again, shunting the auto-train from Caerphilly clear of the main line, on which a Newport to Brecon train is due. Thirty-four years earlier, in the previous photograph, this same movement would have just been carried out to put the PC&N train into the sidings. However, things were about to change. The Pontypridd to Machen passenger service continued to be operated by British Railways only until 17 September 1956, when it was withdrawn. No 6433, with two auto-coaches and carrying a wreath on its smokebox door, made the final journey. *F. Hornby*

Left Machen station, looking in the opposite direction towards Church Road station. Ex-GWR engine No 351, formerly Taff Vale Railway Class 'A' No 91 built in 1921, is seen with auto-trailer No 103 attached, shunting between platforms to form the 7.25pm train back to Caerphilly on 13 September 1951. *R. M. Casserley*

Below left This photograph shows the completed movement, with No 351 at the front and the auto-trailer behind ready to form the 7.25pm to Caerphilly. As it waits for passengers some young enthusiasts are asking question.

Machen station closed to passenger services on 31 December 1962, and finally closed entirely on 16 July 1964. In 1996 it had the abandoned look of neglect. The station buildings were still standing, but gradually falling into disrepair; the wooden waiting room, GWR-inscribed station seat and bordered flower beds are only a memory now, a memory of a once busy and important station. *R. M. Casserley*

Right Extracts from the Taff Vale Railway Rule Book of 1894, relating to working between Machen and Newport. *Courtesy of D. C. Thomas*

Below The dispute between the PC&N and GWR at Bassaleg is settled – an extract from the *Pontypridd Chronicle*, 2 August 1884. *Pontypridd Public Library*

PONTYPRIDD, CAERPHILLY AND NEWPORT RAILWAY.

The mineral traffic on this railway is being gradually developed. The dispute between the Great Western Railway Company and the Pontypridd and Caerphilly Railway Company has been, to a certain extent, settled in such a way as to enable traffic to be sent from the Rhondda Valley to Newport. The running powers of the new railway company do not permit of the Taff Vale engines passing over the Great Western system, although a working arrangement will in all probability be entered into shortly; but the Great Western Company do not object to convey the traffic themselves. The Taff Vale Railway Company convey the mineral trains to Bassaleg Junction, thence they are conveyed to the Alexandra Dock by the engines of the Great Western Railway Company, and these engines return the empty wagons to the place whence they were taken. Under this arrangement several mineral trains are now passing to and fro on the new railway daily.

P. C. & N. and B. & M. RAILWAYS (Con.)

STATIONS AND JUNCTIONS.	TO AND FROM	WHISTLES.	REMARKS.
Church Road	Main Line	1	
	Sidings	2	
	Cross over Road	3	
Rhiwderin	Main Line	1	
	Siding	2	
	Cross over Road	3	
Bassaleg North Box	Up and Down Main	1	
	Down Relief Line	2 and 2 short	
	Down Siding North of Box	3 short and 1 crow	
	New Siding for Up Empties	1 short and 1 crow	
	Cross over Road	1 short and 1 long	
	Up Main and Relief	2 crows	
	,, to Yard	1 and 3 short	
77	Down Main to Yard	6 short	

P. C. & N. and B. & M. RAILWAYS (Con.)

STATIONS AND JUNCTIONS.	TO AND FROM	WHISTLES.	REMARKS.
Bassaleg Station Box	Down Relief to Main Line	2 crows and 2 short	
	Down Main to P. C. & N. Line	3	
	,, to Siding	1 and 1 short	
	Station Cross over	1 crow and 4 short	
	Cross over on Bridge	3 long and 1 crow	
	G.W.R.	2 long	
	No. 1 Siding close to Junction	1 and 1 crow	
	No. 2 Siding close to Junction	1 and 2 crows	
	No. 1 Siding South of Engine Shed	1 crow	
	No. 2 ,, ,, ,,	2 and 1 short and 1 crow	
	No. 3 ,, ,, ,,	1 and 2 short	
	Main Line and Coal Siding	6 short and 1 crow	
	Maesglas Weighing Line	6 long	
78	Engine to take Water on Viaduct	3 crows	

P. C. & N. and B. & M. RAILWAYS (Con.)

STATIONS AND JUNCTIONS.	TO AND FROM	WHISTLES.	REMARKS.
Viaduct Box	Through Trains	1 and 1 short	
Mendalgyffe Junction	To and From Main Line	1	
	Up Line and Storage and vice versa	2	
	Down Line and Storage and vice versa	2 and 1 short	

NOTE.—Special Passenger and Excursion Trains to carry the same Head Marks or Lights as Regular Trains, according to destination.

NOTE.—All engines and trains, including engines and trains of Foreign Companies, working on the Main Line and the various Branches, not otherwise provided for, must carry—
By day, 1 lamp at foot of chimney.
By night, 1 white light in same position.

79

Church Road was the next station along the Brecon & Merthyr line from Machen to Newport High Street station. It is seen here looking towards Rhiwderin circa 1910. The station closed entirely on 16 September 1957; the station building is now in private hands.

Rhiwderin station, on towards Bassaleg, closed to passenger services on 1 March 1954, and to goods on 14 September 1959. It is also now in private ownership and much of its former character has been retained, thanks to the present owners. *Courtesy of* The Railway Magazine, *1918*

The B&M's Bassaleg station, looking towards Newport circa 1910. A through PC&N Newport to Pontypridd service is approaching, operated by GWR staff; it has just crossed the bridge that spans the River Ebbw. Bassaleg station closed to passenger services on 31 December 1962, and to goods traffic on 16 July 1964. Today the platforms are still in good condition, although the waiting room seen here has long gone, and a restaurant has been built on the site of the station buildings. *Lens of Sutton*

From Park Junction, 1 mile from East Mendalgief Junction, Newport, the double-tracked PC&N line ran parallel with the Western Valleys line of the former Monmouth Railway & Canal Company, along a stretch of track known as the 'Golden Mile'. It was this short stretch of line that became infamous due to the fact that all lines to the docks passed through Lord Tredegar's estates, and a levy of 1 penny per ton per mile was charged.

This is Maesglas Junction circa 1900, possibly during the quadrupling of the tracks. Eventually there were six running lines as well as two loop lines that came from the western curve at Maesglas signal box. *T. Jukes*

Above A view of Park Junction, showing former GWR '56' Class 0-6-2T No 5697, built at Swindon in 1927, in British Railways livery with an up valleys freight on 11 March 1959. *S. Rickard*

Right A Brecon & Merthyr 0-6-0 saddle tank engine, one of the double-framed design, seen at Newport station. These sturdy engines were excellent machines, and could be seen working both passenger and goods trains. This example, No 31, is seen with a passenger train on the B&M's Newport to Rhymney service departing from this GWR station circa 1902. These engines were all withdrawn around 1920-21. *Courtesy of* The Railway Magazine, *1913*

Right Platform 4 at Newport station, with an auto-train consisting of a GWR '57' Class pannier tank and Driving Brake 2nd coach No W247W waiting for passengers on 27 May 1956. *F. Hornby*

6. LINES INTO THE DOCKS

PC&N

The line from Bassaleg to the sidings at Mendalgief opened in April 1886. From Bassaleg Junction to Bassaleg Loop, a distance of 6 chains, the line was single track, with the line north of Bassaleg Loop signal box to East Mendalgief Junction being double track, worked by the Tyers Absolute Block system. 'Permissive block' was installed from Bassaleg Junction to Park Junction during the latter part of 1938 because of the installation of crossovers for relief dock lines at Bassaleg Junction. Bassaleg Loop closed to traffic on 3 September 1959.

Beyond Park Junction the line crossed the South Wales main line from Newport to Cardiff by means of overbridges to reach West Mendalgief Junction, from there dropping down the embankment on which the signal box stood to reach Mendalgief East Junction, and from there into the North and South Docks internal lines (see the map on pages 24-5).

The siding serving Lord Tredegar's Park Yard was used for coal deliveries to the house and estate, and was retained until their removal on 7 December 1967. It is fitting that the last piece of track from the PC&N line should come from the former estates of the late Lord Tredegar.

GWR

In 1880 the GWR took over the Monmouth Railway & Canal Company, and this company's traffic from the coalfields of the Western Valleys of Monmouthshire was conveyed towards the ANDR's North Dock, and later the South Dock, over the former MRCC lines. After the GWR took over these lines at the Grouping of 1922, the area was renamed as the Great Western Railway's Monmouthshire & Western Valleys Division.

From West Mendalgief Junction running powers were formerly granted by the GWR to the PC&N for its traffic to run on the former MRCC metals. This junction was rebuilt by the GWR on 3 February 1928, and closed on 20 May 1960.

The line from East Mendalgief Junction, where the ANDR and PC&N lines met, to the GWR's Alexandra Dock Junction on the South Wales main line was opened on 10 April 1875, with running powers granted to the PC&N. In 1896 this junction was resignalled, and became a common conveying point for the rail traffic entering or leaving the Alexandra Docks. A GWR memo dated 26 June 1930, issued from the Chief Dock Manager's Office, Cardiff, describes the situation: 'While the statutory railway of the Alexandra Docks Company terminated at East Mendalgief Junction, between that point and ship's side the traffic had to be hauled for varying distances to and from the respective coal hoists and general cargo quays at the dock… Traffic to and from the Great Western Railway Company was exchanged either at Maesglas Junction or the Alexandra Dock Junction, with the Alexandra Docks Company working the traffic in either direction between these junctions and the ship's side.'

East Mendalgief Junction was closed to traffic on 20 November 1966.

Above right This aerial view of circa 1937 shows the extensive railway network that led into the Alexandra Docks, and can be compared with the map on pages 24-5. 'A' (the white roofs in the middle distance) is the Whitehead Iron & Steel Works, over to the right is 'B', British Briquettes Limited, and next to them is 'C', the works of Messrs Braithwaite & Co (Engineers). In the middle is 'D', the top end of the North Dock, and over to the left is 'E', part of the Timber Float. *Newport County Council*

Right This aerial view gives a closer view of the Whitehead Court-y-Bella Works, circa 1937. To the left of the buildings is the extensive network of the Monmouthshire Bank Sidings. *Author's collection*

Below Coal for shipment abroad circa 1930, shown here at the Tredegar Park Sidings, one of the Alexandra Docks numerous yards. The wagons bearing the initials 'EV' are from the Ebbw Vale collieries, while those marked 'JL' are from the John Lancaster Company, which had collieries at Blaina, Cwmtillery and Griffin. *Associated British Ports*

Opposite top Maesglas Junction was opened on 10 April 1875, and was resignalled in 1896 due to the increased amount of traffic that was entering the Alexandra Docks

from the GWR system at this point. This photograph shows the junction during an SLS railtour visit on 11 July 1959; it was eventually closed on 3 September 1979. *J. J. Davis*

Opposite middle This photograph, looking north-westwards from East Mendalgief Junction circa 1930, shows the sidings towards West Mendalgief on the left and the Monmouthshire Bank sidings on the right. The building on the extreme right might possibly be Monmouthshire Bank Cabin signal box. *Associated British Ports*

Right A special train from the Brown, Lenox Works at Pontypridd entering the Alexandra Docks via the PC&N line in April 1934. The load, which consisted of Admiralty mooring buoys, was eventually shipped out of the docks on 22 April 1934 aboard the SS *Greyfriars* en route to Rosyth in Scotland. The buoys weighed 6 tons 18 cwt each, and measured 13 feet by 10 feet. They are seen here on GWR 'Crocodile B' bogie trolleys, which carried a load of 15 tons. *Associated British Ports*

This photograph, circa 1910, shows the extensive use to which the Storage Sidings were put, and the tremendous amount of sidings needed to accommodate the vast number of private colliery coal wagons that were en route to the west side of the South Docks. *Associated British Ports*

Internal dock lines

The internal dock lines of the ANDR began at East Mendalgief Junction. The Alexandra Docks were at one time served by a continuous procession of wagons and coal trucks, with the sidings providing accommodation extending to upwards of 100 miles in length, and by 1914 covering a ground space of over 50 acres. Also provided free was storage space for the stacking of rails and iron ore for a period of 90 days prior to shipping, when required. By 1932 the storage and siding accommodation had been increased to hold 12,000 wagons.

The Tank Sidings were so called because they were adjacent to a sludge tank, into which the bilge contents of vessels were pumped. These sidings were removed some time in the 1970s. Cork Sidings were used for the storage of cattle, which had been shipped over from Ireland and disembarked at Cork Wharf. Again these were removed in the 1970s. Marshalling Sidings were formerly situated on the west side of North Dock, and were also lifted some time in the early part of the 1970s; they were also known as Storage Sidings.

As can be seen, although there was a complicated amount of junctions and sidings in the maze of lines in the Alexandra Docks complex, the distance between them was not great when compared with other railway companies – but they could be confusing when confronted for the first time!

Seen here are the tracks leading into the docks circa 1910. Those on the left lead to the west side of North Dock, while those going straight on lead to the coal hoists at South Dock. *ANDR booklet of 1916*

Above Deal timber in transit from the ship to the timber yards inside Alexandra Docks circa 1910. *ANDR booklet of 1916*

Below Rolling Bridge Junction, circa 1910. Originally the bridge was hydraulically operated and had a travel of 107 feet, the whole structure being carried on cast iron cylinders 8 feet in diameter with an average depth of 54 feet; a speed of 5mph was imposed on all traffic. After the extension of the track to the Salvage Factory in 1915 the bridge was fixed in position, its new name replacing the former one of Rolling Bridge Crossing. In 1934 the Salvage Factory became No 9 Transit Shed, and extra sidings were laid that same year to

provide accommodation for an extra 671 railway wagons. The photograph shows the bridge from the south. *ANDR booklet of 1916*

Below A letter from the General Manager's Office, Newport Docks, dated 1901, and still showing the original ANDR title 20 years after it was changed to the longer title below. *D. Rees collection*

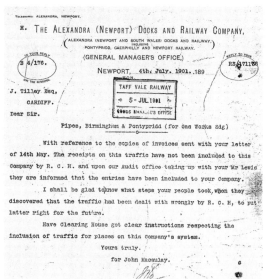

ALEXANDRA
(NEWPORT AND SOUTH WALES)
DOCKS AND RAILWAY.

As issued 5th October 1908

Regulations as to Private Owners' Waggons.

The Alexandra (Newport and South Wales) Docks and Railway Company hereby give notice that the working of Private Owners' Waggons on the Company s Railways is subject to the following Regulations : –

1.—The owners of all new, reconstructed or converted vehicles intended to work upon the Alexandra (Newport and South Wales) Docks and Railway, must, before they are brought into use, communicate with Mr. T. W. R. Pearson, Locomotive and Waggon Superintendent, Alexandra Docks, Newport, Mon., so that he may have them inspected without unreasonable delay, and, if built, reconstructed or converted (as the case may be) in accordance with the Railway Clearing House Standard Specification, register plates, as described in the Specification, shall be forthwith affixed to each.

2 —The name and Address of the Owner or Lessee, the Waggon-number, and the tare, shall be painted conspicuously on both sides of the waggon ; the maximum load must also be clearly indicated on both sides of the waggon.

When waggons are let on hire the Lessee will, for the purpose of these Regulations, be regarded as the Owner.

Provided that when the hire is for a term of not less than three months, the name and address of the Lessee shall be painted or exhibited on a board or plate on both sides of the waggon, and that when the hire is for less than three months, the name and address of the Lessee shall either be so painted, or exhibited on a card (other than the waggon-label), on both sides of the waggon.

3.—The Owners or Lessees, as the case may be, shall keep their waggons in good working condition, and have them properly lubricated and examined and put into good repair before being tendered to the Company for transit.

4 —The Company may remove the register plates from any waggon if wheels, axles or any other materials of less dimensions or strength than those provided for by the Railway Clearing House Standard Specification are afterwards substituted in contravention of the conditions of the said Specification.

5 —If in transit any defect should be observed, which for the proper and safe working it is necessary to repair before the vehicles are allowed to proceed further, the Company may, with the consent of the Owners, make such repairs, and charge them with all expenses incurred in effecting the same.

6.—In pursuance of the rules made by the Board of Trade under the provisions of the Railway Employment (Prevention of Accidents) Act, 1900, when it is necessary in the ordinary course of business that any label or direction as to destination or consignee shall be placed upon any railway waggon, such label or direction must be placed on both sides of such waggon ; and no Private Owner's Waggon will be accepted for conveyance on the Company's railway unless so labelled or directed on both sides.

All waggon Owners, representatives of waggon Companies and their repairers, when labelling defective waggons at railway stations and depôts shall clearly set forth on the labels the station or siding from and to which the waggons are required to travel, and hand in a proper Consignment Note or written forwarding instructions.

7.—When waggons, for the purpose of repair, are required to be shunted into and out of Railway companies sidings and/or into and out of premises in the occupation of [Private Waggon Repairers a charge of 6d. per waggon will be made for such services, except where a higher charge is now made, in which case such higher charge shall be the maximum charge under these regulations.

Siding rent will be chargeable to the Owner, or his agent, in respect of standing room for any waggon detained at a station or siding for repairs at the rate of 6d. per waggon per day, which will be calculated from the expiration of three days, exclusive of the date of the advice note, Sundays and Bank Holidays, from the time the waggon is placed at the disposal of the Owner or Repairer, and to terminate when the waggon is labelled for despatch after repair.

8.—Any authorised servant of the Company may detain any waggon which may appear to him unfit to run until it has been put into proper repair and passed by one of the Company's waggon examiners or inspectors.

9.—The Company will not be responsible for any damage to Private Owners' Waggons left unprotected in an imperfect state by the Owners, nor for any injury that may occur to waggon repairers, who will be required to execute an indemnity before they are allowed to work on the Company's premises.

10.—Private Owners' Waggons running over the Railway Company's lines must not, apart from a reasonable description of the contents of the waggon, be used for advertising purposes, but the Railway Company will not object to a description (to be approved by them) of a product of the Owner's manufacture being painted thereon.

11.—*Nothing contained in these Regulations shall prejudice or affect any legal liability to each other of the actual Owners or Lessees of Waggons and the Railway Companies.*

JOHN MACAULAY,
General Manager.

Newport, Mon.,
October, 1908.

S A.—28431.   K6.11.

'Regulations as to Private Owners' Waggons', October 1908. *Associated British Ports*

7. LOCOMOTIVES AND ROLLING-STOCK

Steam railmotors

Below Railmotor No 1, which was built by the Glasgow Railway & Engineering Co Ltd, Govan, Glasgow, in 1904, and fitted with 3-foot disc wheels. This photograph shows ANDR Company staff and officials during the railmotor's acceptance trials of 1 September 1904, quite an important occasion. *Welsh Industrial & Maritime Museum, Cardiff*

Right An interior view of Railmotor No 1 circa 1904, showing the seating capacity for 52 passengers. The overall length of the railmotor was 55ft 6in, and this seating arrangement lasted until 1911, when it was rebuilt into an ordinary carriage with seating for 68 passengers. After the Grouping the railmotor was renumbered as coach No 95. On 1 September 1928 it was transferred to service stock as loco workman's coach No 173, finally being withdrawn from service on 22 September 1934. *Associated British Ports*

Railcar No 2 of 1905, which was also built by Glasgow Railway & Engineering. It had an overall length of 61ft 3in, and like No 1 was also rebuilt, to carry 58 passengers. On 1 September 1923 the GWR renumbered it as coach No 90, and it was finally withdrawn from service on 25 October 1930. This railcar had a clerestory roof, and is seen here at the Alexandra Docks after purchase in 1905. *Associated British Ports*

Steam locomotives

Most of the Alexandra Docks engines had short 0-6-0 or 0-4-0 wheelbases and were of the saddle or pannier design, which was essential for dock working, especially with the tight curvature of the internal lines presenting the ever-present danger of a derailment, which could not only cause serious injury but would also cause unwanted delay and loss of revenue.

Today the types of engines that work inside the docks are former British Rail 08 Class diesel shunters, reliable workhorses in their own right.

Trojan, an 0-4-0 saddle tank engine, in use at the Alder Paper Mill at Tamworth. It was built in 1897 by the Avonside Engine Company to work with 0-4-0 engine *Alexandra* (see opposite) in the Town Dock. After the Grouping the GWR did not want these non-standard engines, so in July 1934 *Trojan* was withdrawn and sold to the Moira Colliery, then to the Victoria Colliery, Wellington. Finally in December 1947 it was transferred to the Alder Paper Mills. Apart from the removal of the chimney cap, the substitution of a deeper-toned whistle and the extension of the cab side sheet, this engine was almost in its original condition when photographed with its GWR number 1340 on 22 April 1958. *R. M. Casserley*

Right ANDR 0-4-0 *Alexandra*, seen here with its GWR number 1341 at the former Taff Vale Railway's yard at Cathays, Cardiff, on 11 May 1927; by the look of the background scene, it is next to the Woodville Road bridge. *Alexandra* was built in 1884 by Hawthorn Leslie at its works at Newcastle-upon-Tyne. It was withdrawn from service in 1946 and cut up at Caerphilly engine shed in July of that year. *R. M. Casserley*

Left Seen here at Newport is ANDR engine No 1, photographed with its driver and fireman on 31 July 1905. It was an 0-6-0 saddle tank built by Robert Stephenson in 1898. Later it was renumbered by the GWR as 674, and was withdrawn from service in 1929. *LCGB (Ken Nunn Collection)*

Below ANDR No 3, another 0-6-0 saddle tank photographed at the Alexandra Docks on 31 July 1905. This engine was also built by Robert Stephenson, in 1900, renumbered by the GWR as 676, and finally withdrawn in 1929. *LCGB (Ken Nunn Collection)*

Above Engine No 7, named by the ANDR as *Pontypridd*, one of the company's coal train engines. Built by Sharpe in 1857, it was originally purchased by the London & North Western Railway (LNWR) and is seen here at Pontypridd in 1884. It was eventually withdrawn from service in 1900. *Welsh Industrial & Maritime Museum, Cardiff*

ANDR engine No 9, with attendant staff. This Beyer Peacock engine was built in 1887 and was one of those purchased by the ANDR in November/December 1903 from the former Mersey Railway Company. It was with this engine that the submerged coal trials and experiments were carried out (see below). Renumbered by the GWR as 1211, it was withdrawn in 1929. It is seen here just after delivery, probably in 1904. Syren and Shipping *magazine*

Experiments with submerged coal

Early this century an article by Lord Charles Beresford appeared in *The Times* newspaper, concerning the marked loss of calorific power in coal that was stored for naval use at coaling stations abroad, and thus the loss of power to the Royal Navy's vessels.

Shortly after reading this article ANDR General Manager Mr Macauley noted that the dredger at work alongside one of the coal hoists was bringing up an occasional lump of coal that had tumbled into the water during the course of shipping. He was struck with the idea that the storage of coal under water might enable the calorific value to be retained, perhaps better than when exposed to the air.

Enquiries were promptly set in hand as to the general quality of any coal that had been recovered from the ANDR docks. It was found that when any available quantity worth separating from the mud was recovered, it was used for minor purposes during the winter periods by the men working around the docks. To the amazement of some, far from having deteriorated it was found that this coal was better – it burned more cleanly, and gave a better flame.

One example was a small furnace that was kept burning day and night near the Alexandra Docks engine shed for the purpose of drying sand for locomotive use; occasionally a shovelful of live coals was used to assist in the making up of a locomotive fire after the cleaning-out process. A quantity of small dredged coal was from time to time burned and found to be particularly good.

To a certain extent comparison was practicable at this initial stage, for the sweepings around the hoists were also used at this furnace, and the coal that had been under water was found to be far superior, and was always greeted with joy by the stoker when available. In short, the coal that had been under water for some time was far superior to that mined within a week of being used, both being in the same physical state, ie 'small'.

The coal recovered from the dock had been under water for a period of between six to nine months. It had been impossible to dredge it sooner, and then only on Sundays unless absolutely necessary, owing to the great pressure of work during 1901-4, with the demand for hoists and the handling of coal shipments.

Mr Macauley was pleased with the results, as far as they went, but it was decided that they did not go far enough to enable a firm conclusion to be made. For instance, in the case of 'small' coal the improved results may have been due to the washing that the coal may have received, by which an amount of less valuable dust would have been washed away; on the other hand, a considerable proportion of the dredged coal could have been nothing more than dust, which, falling upon the surface of the water in the process of tipping had settled as sediment to the dock bottom.

The result of these findings and thoughts was that a series of tests were performed to get more accurate results, then they were again repeated even more carefully and elaborately. In the light of the experience gained a selected ANDR engine and crew were picked out for a series of practical experiments upon the company's railway between Pontypridd and Newport. The fullest records of the work carried out continuously on the footplate of the engine were carefully made and analysed, with every precaution taken to arrive at the correct result.

Laboratory experiments were able to confirm the practical tests, that coal known to have been submerged for periods ranging from one to three years would lose between 1 and 2 per cent of its calorific value, whereas coal exposed to air would lose from 10 to 12 per cent in this country, and in foreign stations having a higher temperature, especially if exposed to wind, probably nearly twice that amount. The lower loss with the submerged coal was held to be due to protection from oxidation by the enveloping water and the physical weathering effects of the sun, wind, rain and frost, and lastly by the more complete retention in the innumerable fissures of steam coal of its more volatile constituents, giving it a high burning value. It was also found that these results did not apply to any other type of coal other than Welsh; other varieties, being harder, lost far less through exposure to air.

The experiments had been carried out not to find a comparison between the keeping qualities of different coals, but to arrive at the best method of overcoming the pronounced tendency of Welsh coal – the best steam-raising coal in the world – to dissipate its energy upon exposure to the air. Welsh coal was a 'fuller' type and could hold the constituents necessary for producing power 'in the vein'; this conclusion was clear from the calorific degradation that commenced in the colliery itself, represented by the inflammable gases being given off, and against which many elaborate precautions had to be taken in the fiery seams of the South Wales coalfields.

Above ANDR engine No 12, seen here 31 July 1905 at the Alexandra Docks, was built by R. W. Hawthorn and sold to the ANDR in 1884. After the Grouping it was renumbered by the GWR as 664, and was withdrawn from the Alexandra Docks in 1930. By 1940 it had been sold to the Seaton Burn Colliery in the Northumberland coalfields, which renumbered it as SBC No 1. *LCGB (Ken Nunn Collection)*

Left ANDR No 13 with its crew circa 1884. This 0-6-0 saddle tank was also purchased from R. W. Hawthorn in 1884, and is seen here 'as new' at the Alexandra Docks. It was withdrawn in September 1926. *Welsh Industrial & Maritime Museum, Cardiff*

Left In 1917 the last of the two steam railmotors was withdrawn. As all coaches were now required to be loco-hauled, an extra engine was purchased to work the PC&N line. This was a former GWR 0-4-2T of the '517' Class, No 1426, which was renumbered 14 by the ANDR. This picturesque scene shows No 14 with its trailer coach picking up passengers at Groeswen circa 1917. *The Oakwood Press*

Top ANDR No 17, another 0-6-0 design, photographed at the Hawthorn Leslie Works at Newcastle-upon-Tyne on 29 April 1920. Renumbered 672 by the GWR, it did not last long with its new owners, being withdrawn in 1924. After withdrawal its boiler was rebuilt in 1927 and fitted to former ANDR engine No 16, which extended the latter's working life for a further ten years. *LCGB (Ken Nunn Collection)*

Middle This view of former ANDR engine No 19 (right) shows it with its new GWR number 680 outside Oswestry shed next to GWR 2-4-0T No 617 on 31 May 1932. No 19 was built by Peckett & Sons in 1886, and after the Grouping, as No 680, it spent the rest of its life working from Oswestry shed. *R. M. Casserley*

Bottom ANDR 0-6-4T No 22 was purchased from the Mersey Railway Company, and is seen here at the Alexandra Docks on 5 August 1905. Note that it is still in Mersey Railway livery and has a painted on number. Built by Beyer Peacock in 1885, it did not last long after the Grouping; renumbered by the GWR as 1344, it was withdrawn in 1923. Documents show that the heaviest coal trains were given to the company's three 0-6-4 tank engines, Nos 22, 23 and 24, with loads from Caerphilly and Bassaleg en route to the Alexandra Docks consisting of 70 wagons. *LCGB (Ken Nunn Collection)*

Top   Seen here alongside other scrapped engines is ANDR 0-6-4T No 24, another of the Beyer Peacock engines of 1885, renumbered by the GWR as 1346 and withdrawn in 1927. It was photographed on the Swindon scrap lines on 11 September of that year. *R. M. Casserley*

Middle   ANDR 0-6-0 No 28 at the Alexandra Docks sidings circa 1909 (sometimes this photograph has been referred to as being at the Interchange Sidings, Pontypridd). No 28 was built at the GWR's Swindon Works in 1886, and remained in PC&N service for many years, being one of a pair of GWR '1661' Class engines purchased by the ANDR in 1906. After the Grouping it was renumbered 1683, and was finally withdrawn from service in 1926. The two Barnum & Bailey coaches, sometimes referred to as Pullman coaches, were purchased by the ANDR in 1909 (see page 127). *Pontypridd Public Library*

Bottom   This 0-6-0 saddle tank was built by the GWR at its Wolverhampton Works in 1875 as No 993, and was purchased by the ANDR in 1913 and given the number 33. After the Grouping the GWR again renumbered it 993, and it was withdrawn in 1930. It is seen here in 1913 on one of the docks' numerous sidings. *Welsh Industrial & Maritime Museum, Cardiff*

Above 2-6-2T No 1205 passes Canton Sheds, Cardiff, on 10 September 1951. This Hawthorn Leslie engine of 1920 was one of the last built for the ANDR, which numbered it 36. A powerful 2-6-2 'Prairie' tank, it could haul heavy coal trains yet was able to negotiate the sharp curves of the docks. Renumbered by the GWR as 1205, it was withdrawn from service in 1956. *R. M. Casserley*

Right Driver Reg Young and Fireman O'Shea in the cab of engine No 3714 pulling the last through train from Pontypridd to Newport, photographed here at platform 7 of Newport station at 8.35am on 15 September 1956 (see also page 101). This GWR engine was built in 1936 and was allocated to Newport Ebbw Junction engine shed until withdrawal in 1963. *S. C. L. Phillips and D. K. Jones*

Pill engine sheds

The ANDR only had three engine sheds: one was at Glyntaff near to the goods depot there, the second was situated on the east side of the land that was lost when South Dock was excavated, and the third was at Pill, part of the docks complex.

Pill engine shed was opened by the ANDR in 1898, and was enlarged by the GWR to handle the extra engines that were transferred there when Newport Dock Street and Bassaleg engine sheds were closed. These closures were caused by the declining coal trade which brought with it the closure of the Town Dock and less traffic for the railways. The GWR also added extra coaling facilities in 1929. Access to this shed was gained via East Mendalgief Junction.

A feature of Pill was the grounded coach bodies used as mess rooms, offices and storeroom facilities. One of these was originally a fairly typical Edwardian non-corridor coach, but the other was of a type that most of us have only seen in Wild West films, described by the GWR as an American parlour car with 'end verandah'.

Pill was given the shed code 86B by British Railways in 1949. When the shed closed in June 1963 the engines allocated there were transferred to the nearby Ebbw Junction shed.

ANDR engine No 18, an 0-6-0 saddle tank, photographed outside Pill engine sheds on 31 July 1905. *LCGB (Ken Nunn Collection)*

Left Former Alexandra Docks engine No 16, rebuilt and renumbered by the GWR as 671, at Pill on 27 August 1931. This engine, withdrawn from service by the GWR in 1937, is hauling steel-bodied GWR coal wagons, possibly en route for engine shed use. *D. K. Jones*

Below No 666 at Pill shed on 4 May 1951. In the background can be seen one of the grounded coach bodies in use as a store or mess room. *R. M. Casserley*

GWR staff pose alongside Alexandra Dock shunting engine No 667 (GWR) circa 1927. This engine was formerly ANDR No 34, built at the Kerr Stuart Works in 1917, and was withdrawn from service by British Railways in 1954. In the cab are driver W. H. Walters and fireman Gregory; also in the photograph are Billie Davies, Joe Burgess and Ivor Harris. *Courtesy of Miss M. Parsons, granddaughter of the late W. H. Walters*

Barnum & Bailey coaches

After touring the United States for many years, in 1896 James Bailey of Barnum & Bailey's Circus decided to tour Great Britain; his partner for many years, Phineas T. Barnum, had died a few years earlier. Because of loading gauge restrictions imposed on their American-made carriages and rolling-stock, a contract was agreed with W. R. Renshaw & Company of the Phoenix Works, Stoke-on-Trent, to build the stock required for the tour.

ANDR coach No 1, one of the former Barnum & Bailey Circus coaches purchased by the ANDR in 1910 for use on its Pontypridd, Caerphilly and Newport line, and seen after delivery. One of the first jobs that had to be carried out on these coaches was treatment for the removal of lice, an inheritance from their circus days. The coach had a total length of 54ft 6in. Its two four-wheeled bogies had a 7-foot wheelbase and were fitted with small 28-inch-diameter wheels; the floor was 11 inches lower than the British standard. Barnum & Bailey's Circus appeared at Cardiff on 21-24 June 1899, travelling on to Newport and opening there on 26 June, before moving onwards to Gloucester the next day. It is quite possible that members of the ANDR Board of Directors visited the circus and saw with interest the coaches and rolling-stock being used. It must have been quite an eye-opener in many ways! *His Honour Judge Watkin Powell*

Above This interior view of ANDR coach No 1 in 1910 shows padded seats rather than the usual wooden slatted type of seating that would be used for 3rd Class accommodation by other railway companies. One of the coaches was used as a stationary office at Pill engine sheds from 1920, and was officially withdrawn from service in 1923; the other two were taken out of service in 1926, one of them (possibly No 3) going into storage as condemned stock at Foss Cross on the former Midland & South Western Junction Railway. The other coach survived in departmental use with the GWR until 1934. This and the previous photograph are part of a collection on permanent loan from His Honour Judge Watkin Powell to the Welsh Industrial & Maritime Museum, Cardiff. *His Honour Judge Watkin Powell*

Below left ANDR coach No 3, withdrawn by the GWR in 1926, awaiting restoration at the Welsh Industrial & Maritime Museum, Cardiff, on 29 October 1988. It was discovered lying in a field in Devon, having been nearly broken up and burned by its former owner. Much work has still be to done, but given time this coach will resume its former character. *Author*

Right The elephant cars sold to the ANDR were numbered 104 and 105. This is No 105 with the British design of buffers and couplings seen at the left-hand end; the other end would have had the American buckeye type fitted. Elephant car No 104 would have had the wood-panelled sides reaching down to cover the well frame, almost to rail level, but as can be seen on No 105 it does not reach down so far. A common feature of these Barnum & Bailey vans was that the roof was rounded more than is usual, to meet the British loading gauge standards. As with all the Barnum & Bailey circus vehicles, the floor of these elephant cars was built 11 inches lower than the British standard, and they had 7-foot-wheelbase bogies and small 28-inch-diameter wheels. The photograph was taken at the Alexandra Docks, possibly on the day the vehicles were received, 2 September 1910. *Associated British Ports*

Right Elephant car No 105 rebuilt as ANDR Transit Car No 1 in September 1910, a miracle of reconstruction that took less than three weeks. *Associated British Ports*

Renshaw completed the initial contract for 68 assorted vehicles, and later others were to follow, based on the American design and painted in yellow with red lettering for the rolling-stock, and in dark lake with gold lettering for the passenger coaches. 'Barnum & Bailey, the Greatest Show on Earth' was ready to roll.

The first show was at Olympia, London, on 27 December 1897, and at the end of that season, on 12 November 1898, the circus had visited 72 towns. The second season began on 10 April 1899 and lasted until 11 November, visiting 112 towns before crossing the English Channel to Europe.

Colonel 'Buffalo Bill' Cody then hired 50 of these vehicles from Bailey and another tour was started; 'Buffalo Bill's Wild West Show' began on 26

December 1902, again at Olympia. By 1906 the tour was over and Cody returned to American, having toured not only Great Britain but also Europe.

The coaches and rolling-stock were sold to Mr E. E. Cornforth of Trentham, Stoke-on-Trent, who disposed of 23 flat cars, two elephant cars and three passenger coaches to the ANDR in 1910. Two of the flat cars were fitted with British-type couplings at Renshaw's works to enable the movement of the complete batch of 28 vehicles from Stoke-on-Trent to the Alexandra Docks as one train. The passenger coaches retained their end balconies, but with the ANDR initials incorporated in wrought iron, while the underframe storage boxes were removed at Renshaw's before departure.

8. SIGNAL BOXES

Movement of the mineral traffic from the Rhondda and Cynon Valleys via Pontypridd station on the PC&N lines en route to Newport Docks was controlled by the PCN Junction signal box, which came into use in June 1883 for construction purposes in connection with the new line. It was situated at the southern end of Pontypridd station, and had closed entirely by 16 June 1970.

The line from PCN Junction to Penrhos Junction was double track and was worked by the Absolute Block system. The first signal box was Interchange Sidings, opened in 1888; it closed in 1906 when, on 1 May, a new signal box was opened, known as Interchange Sidings West; this box closed in 1941. The Board of Trade inspection report dated 28 April 1906 stated that the old PC&N

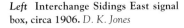

Left **Interchange Sidings East signal box, circa 1906.** *D. K. Jones*

Right Groeswen signal box, with members of the permanent way gang in attendance, in 1900. On the extreme left can be seen a cross carved into the embankment; possibly in remembrance of the death of a colleague or a beloved pet, it remains a mystery, the answer hidden by time. *Pontypridd Public Library*

Interchange Sidings signal box and the old connections with it were to be removed, and that the new Interchange Sidings signal box would contain 38 working and 12 spare levers. Glyntaff signal box would contain 32 working and 10 spare levers, and at each of these signal boxes, which were located on a very high embankment, some protective railing would be required at the side of the cabin to prevent accidents to the signalmen. By 9 April 1908 the new Interchange Sidings West signal box contained 39 working levers and 3 spares.

Glyntaff signal box was located south of the Glamorganshire Canal bridge, and was replaced by a new signal box on the north side of the bridge in 1906; this was Interchange Sidings East signal box, which closed on 28 January 1962, to be replaced by a ground frame. It was also on that day that the line from PCN Junction to Penrhos Junction was singled. The area once covered by the interchange sidings and Brown, Lenox's sidings is now part of the Pontypridd bypass.

Pontypridd Gas Works Siding signal box opened in 1897. The original agreement, dated 24 April 1895, was for the construction of the siding. On 16 September 1926 this box closed and a ground frame was installed to work the siding. On 23 May 1954 both siding and ground frame were taken out of use.

Dynea signal box opened in 1895 and closed in 1900. Groeswen signal box opened in January 1900, on the down side of the line, and was replaced by a box of a different design, but on the same site, in 1901. I have not seen any proof, either written or photographic, but there may have been a box located on the up side from 1899 until 1900. Groeswen signal box was 2m 63ch from Glyntaff, and 1m 55ch from Penrhos. The colliery sidings at Groeswen served the Groeswen and Penygroes collieries; the latter had closed by the turn of the century. A private siding agreement dated 21 August 1899 with Groeswen colliery was replaced by another dated 28 October 1902 with Groeswen & Caradog Collieries Ltd, while another dated 19 April 1902 was with the South Wales United Collieries, ie Groeswen and Caradog. By 29 June 1918 the colliery had closed, and an amendment of that date changed Groeswen Colliery to read Groeswen Siding; these sidings were removed in 1924. Water columns were provided on the up and down lines adjacent to the overbridge, hence the large tank situated on the bank above the signal box.

Beyond Caerphilly, Gwaun-y-Bara Junction marked the beginning of the new PC&N Machen Loop, for use by down trains, which opened on 14 September 1891. A temporary signal box was opened here in 1888, in connection with the doubling, then a permanent box was opened in 1901, which closed on 25 March 1956. This new line passed Waterloo Halt and joined the main Brecon & Merthyr line at Machen Junction, while trains travelling up this line passed White Hart Halt, which had platforms on both up and down lines, and Fountain Bridge Halt, before crossing the Rhymney River to reach Gwaun-y-Bara Junction. In 1981 the remains of this box were in the garden of the Graig-yr-Rhacca crossing-keeper's house.

The first Bassaleg GWR Junction box closed in 1899, to be replaced by another of the same name but in a different position; this box had closed by 9 December 1968. The PC&N Bassaleg Loop signal box closed on 16 August 1925 when the junction was altered. The B&M Bassaleg South signal box opened in 1898, and closed in 1900.

Park Junction signal box, opened in October 1882, was of a McKenzie & Holland design. It was extended in 1899 to take a 105-lever frame; this was replaced in 1920 by the present 100-lever frame, and the box is still in use today. The complex layout was much reduced during 1981, and the remodelling resulted in some semaphore signals being replaced by colour lights and a much reduced number of levers in the signal box frame.

The ANDR-built East Mendalgief box was in existence in 1880, but there is no evidence to say when it was built; however, a new 90-lever frame was installed by the GWR in 1926. Because it was an all-timber box, during the Second World War brickwork was added up to window level to protect it from blast damage. It closed in October 1976.

Court-y-bella signal box was replaced by a new box in October 1923, and Pill Bank Junction signal box closed on 24 November 1963.

Inside the docks the Marshalling Sidings ground frame was situated at the junction of the lines leading to the west side of North Dock and those running behind the Timber Floats, to serve coal hoists Nos 18, 19 and 20 in South Dock. Rolling Bridge signal box was located on the north side of the bridge across the original South Lock, later renamed East Lock, opened in 1909. The movement of the bridge was interlocked with the railway signals and road barriers on both sides of the bridge. Rolling Bridge box also contained the levers that lifted the bridge to a height of 4ft 2½in. The weight to be lifted was 450 tons, and the time taken for the lift was 1 minute.

Below left Maesglas Junction signal box, photographed during an SLS railtour visit to the Alexandra Docks complex on 11 July 1959. *J. J. Davis*

Right Gwaun-y-Bara Junction signal box as it looked in the 1950s. It closed on 26 March 1956 and today little is left to show where the signal box or track was; only a slight rise of grass-covered earth and an occasional glimpse of ballast gives away its position. *Courtesy of the late T. B. Sands*

Right The approach roads to the Rolling Bridge, or East Lock Bridge, seen from the north. On the right of the bridge can be seen Rolling Bridge signal box. *Associated British Ports*

Below Park Junction signal box photographed in August 1988. This GWR-built box controlled the immense volume of traffic that used Newport Docks via the junctions near Pye Corner at Bassaleg and Park Junction. Today only two lines are used. *Author*

9. STAFF AND MANAGEMENT

Below On 28 May 1868 Lady Tredegar performed the ceremony of the cutting of the first sod that officially started the excavation of the Alexandra North Dock, under the expert guidance of engineer-in-charge Mr Abernethy. The dock was opened on 13 April 1875, but the public rejoicing was greatly marred by the serious illness of the Chairman, the first Lord Tredegar, whose chair was kept vacant throughout the banquet and celebrations. He died on the 16th, and was succeeded by his son, the Honourable Godfrey Charles Morgan (pictured here in about 1900).

Sir Godfrey was born at Ruperra Castle in 1831. He served with the 17th Lancers during the Crimean War, attaining the rank of Captain, and was one of the few survivors from the 'Charge of the Light Brigade' at Balaclava. Years later when his gallant steed Sir Briggs died it was buried in the grounds of Tredegar House, Newport, along with his Skye terrier Peeps. From 1858 until 1875 Sir

Godfrey was a Member of Parliament, serving as the elected Conservative member for Brecknockshire. When he became Lord Tredegar in 1875 he inherited estates in Brecknockshire, Glamorganshire and Monmouthshire, a total of over 40,000 acres. He became Colonel of the Monmouth Engineer Militia in 1885, as well as patron for the University College of South Wales and Monmouthshire. He died on 11 March 1913.

The board of the ANDR, of which the second Lord Tredegar was Chairman with 60 shares, also included Sir George Elliot (50 shares), Mr Frank McClean (50), Mr E. M. Underdown (10), Mr G. W. Elliot (10) and Mr J. C. Parkinson (10). The other shareholders were Mr G. P. Bidder (10), Mr Robert Griffin (five), Mr Charles Rose (five), Mr Abernethy (one), Mr Carlisle (one), Mr Markby (one), and Mr Burt (one). Syren and Shipping *magazine*

Above right Mr John Macaulay was the General Manager of the ANDR from 1901 until 1 May 1913. He was born in Edinburgh in 1853 and entered the service of the North British Railway in 1866, at the age of only 13. In 1874 he transferred to the Cheshire Lines Committee, and subsequently became Superintendent at the Brunswick Dock station, Liverpool, remaining there for ten years. In 1894 he became Traffic Manager of the Mersey Tunnel Railway, and during his first six years he increased that company's profits by £6,000 per year. He also introduced and pioneered the use of electrification on that line. During his career he held posts as a Justice of the Peace for Monmouthshire, became a member and Chairman of the Newport Harbour & Pilotage Commissioners, and an associate of the Institute of Civil Engineers, as well as being appointed to a seat on the Board of the former Mold & Denbigh Railway Company.

Mr Macaulay was also an author. His work entitled *Modern Railway Works*, published in 1912, was a very descriptive engineering book.

Mr Macauley's Personal Clerk was Frank Brown, who had entered the service of the London & North Western Railway at Euston in 1896, where he undertook five years of station and traffic work before leaving to join the ANDR. In 1903 he became Parliamentary and Staff Clerk to the General Manager, and in 1908 organised the Company Staff Department and became the Secretary for the ANDR's side on Conciliation Boards.

In March 1916 he became assistant to the General Manager of the ANDR, Mr J. H. Vickery; on the amalgamation with the GWR at the Grouping, the latter was appointed Chief Docks Manager, with Mr Brown as his Assistant. Syren and Shipping *magazine*

Below right J. H. Vickery. In *The Railway Magazine* of 1922 a short article appeared on Mr Vickery, quoted here with the permission of the editor: 'Mr John Herbert Vickery was the General Manager of the ANDR Company at the time of amalgamation into the Great Western Railway, and was offered a new position as the Chief Docks Manager for the GWR Company, his headquarters becoming the Pierhead Building at Bute Docks, Cardiff.

'Mr Vickery gained his experience during the course of a varied career with the London & South Western Railway, beginning as a junior clerk in the goods department and serving therein for eight years in various capacities, later becoming Chief Clerk on the LSWR, in succession to Sir Sam Fay, and for many years acted as the Honourable Secretary to the London & South Western Railway Servants Orphanage, and Vice President of the LSW Railway Servants Temperance Union.

'In March 1913 he was selected to succeed Mr John Macaulay as the General Manager of the ANDR. As well as his railway duties he was also a Magistrate, President of the Newport Development Association and Chairman of the Bristol Channel Dockowners Association.' *Courtesy of The Railway Magazine, 1913*

Left An illuminated memorial presented to J. H. Vickery on behalf of various bodies connected with Newport Docks congratulating him on his appointment to the post of Chief Docks Manager of the GWR. *Associated British Ports*

The Chairman and Board of Directors of the ANDR from 17 June 1914 until 18 June 1919. In the centre on the right is Stanley Baldwin MP, who died in 1947 after a long and honourable career in politics, holding the post of Prime Minister three times. *Associated British Ports*

Members of the ANDR's police force, circa 1916. *Associated British Ports*

Top The ANDR's lock gate staff at East Lock, circa 1914. *Associated British Ports*

Middle A very faded photograph of the ANDR Docks Strike Committee, circa 1911-12. Back row, left to right: C. Lawrence, R. Roberts, J. Fennesey, J. Landers. Third row: W. J. Baker, J. Collins, J. Murray, M. Hardy, C. Dyer, J. Kiley, M. Lynch, D. Driscoll, J. Morgan. Second row: W. Jones, J. O'Brien, A. Gould, C. Evans, J. Barber, F. Broad, P. Knight, G. Lovatt, A. Collins. Front row: J. Lynch, J. McAuley, J. K. Price, J. O'Leary, A. J. Kenny, J. Cadogan, G. Jackson, H. Seer, T. Sunday, F. Woolen, J. Bragg.

Just visible above them is the motto of the Strike Committee, taken from the Bible (Ecclesiastes, Chapter 9, Verse 10): 'Whatsoever thy hand findeth to do, do it with thy might.' *Courtesy of Starling Press Publishers*

PUBLIC NOTICE.

The Alexandra Newport and South Wales Dock and Railway Co. hereby give notice that in consequence of the Coal Strike their goods train between Newport and Pontypridd will be discontinued on and from Monday next, 18th inst., and no goods can be accepted for conveyance until further notice.

JOHN MACAULAY, General Manager.

Above An announcement regarding the strike in the *Pontypridd Observer*, 23 March 1912.

Bottom The ANDR rugby team, photographed on 30 April 1920 after beating the Town Hall staff by one try, which was scored by M. Trew. Back row, left to right: A. J. Coles, S. B. Macay, A. Thomas, W. R. Jones, H. J. Williams, H. Smith, H. J. Gray, T. J. B. Cole, T. W. Mitchell, W. H. Victory, W. Sweet (linesman). Middle row: I. H. Gray, M. Trow, C. Channing, G. F. Jones, R. Dixon (Captain), H. R. Parfitt, L. Taylor, W. J. Martin (referee). Front row: W. Coakham, H. Edmunds, W. Lewis. *Associated British Ports*

The Alexandra (Newport & South Wales) Docks & Railway Company amalgamated with the Great Western Railway Company, Docks Department, on 25 March 1922. The company handed over 39 engines, 652 open goods wagons, nine brake-vans, six covered goods vans and 32 special wagons.

The GWR became part of British Railways upon nationalisation in 1948, and its Docks Department was passed on to the Docks & Inland Waterways Board, which in 1982 formed part of the Associated British Ports group.

This group photograph was taken outside the South Lock Power Station and shows the managerial staff of the ANDR at the time of the take-over by the GWR at the Grouping of 1922. *Courtesy of the late Arthur Wallis*

APPENDIX 1.
PRESERVATION

The former ANDR coach No 3 can now be seen at the Welsh Industrial & Maritime Museum, at Butetown, Cardiff, South Glamorgan. Originally built for the Barnum & Bailey Circus to a standard American design, and later used by Buffalo Bill Cody's Wild West Show, it toured all over Great Britain and Europe. Together with other items of rolling-stock the coach was purchased by the ANDR in 1910 for use on its Pontypridd, Caerphilly and Newport line as part of its railmotor trailer sets. It was transported to the museum in December 1985 from its last resting place near Totnes in Devon.

The ANDR locomotive *Trojan*, currently owned by Mr John B. True, can be seen at the Great Western Society, Didcot Railway Centre, Didcot, Oxfordshire. It is gradually being restored; much has been done so far, with new buffers of Avonside design fitted, a rolling chassis on order, and hopefully a new boiler to be fitted some time in the future.

Above right ANDR coach No 3 awaiting restoration at the Welsh Industrial & Maritime Museum, Cardiff, on 29 October 1988. *Author*

Right Tredegar House and Country Park, Newport, Gwent, the home of the Lords Tredegar from 1402 until 1962. It was taken over by Newport Borough Council in 1974, and has since been refurbished and much restored. Visitors will find the grounds, craft workshops, barns, mill, sunken garden, orangery, and tours of the house itself fascinating, with much on show regarding the history of this famous and respected family. The stable courtyard has recently undergone restoration and this will do much to add to the ornate splendour of the house. *Author*

APPENDIX 2.
ORDNANCE SURVEY MAP
REFERENCE NUMBERS

A present-day listing of all traceable halts, stations, sidings and junctions on the PC&N, Rhymney, Brecon & Merthyr and GWR lines into Newport's Alexandra Docks, with their respective Ordnance Survey map references.

PC&N line

PCN Junction, Pontypridd	ST072898
Broadway railway bridge, Pontypridd	ST073898
Tram Road Halt	ST073898
PC&N viaduct over River Taff	ST074898
Brown, Lenox works siding	ST076898
	to ST079900
Interchange Sidings, West Junction	ST078898
Interchange Sidings, East Junction	ST084896
Glyntaff goods depot	ST085896
Glyntaff Halt	ST084896
Treforest Halt	ST086894
Cemetery Road bridge	ST086893
Glyntaff Gasworks Siding	ST089890
'High Level' Rhydyfelin Halt	ST091888
'GWR' Rhydyfelin Halt	ST093886
Dynea Halt	ST098883
Upper Boat Halt	ST108875
Groeswen Halt	ST115868
Railway bridge over track	ST118863
Railway bridge over stream	ST123861
Nantgarw Halt	ST124858
Nantgarw cattle creep	ST127857
Nantgarw roadbridge	ST128857

Rhymney Railway

Penrhos Junction	ST130857
Barry Railway viaduct abutments	ST136860
Penrhos South Junction	ST139862
Beddau North Junction	ST144863
Caerphilly, Watford Crossing	ST148864
Caerphilly, West Junction	ST153866
Caerphilly station	ST157865
Caerphilly East Junction (with B&M line)	ST161865

Brecon & Merthyr Railway

Caerphilly East Junction	ST161865
Caerphilly Van Road railway bridge	ST163867
Gwern-y-Domen Halt	ST177879
Gwaun-y-Bara Junction	ST179879
Viaduct over River Rhymney (site of)	ST190885
Fountain Bridge Halt	ST191885
Newport Road railway bridge	ST191885
Waterloo Halt	ST195883
Viaduct over River Rhymney	ST201888
	to ST202889
Viaduct crossing river	ST203889
White Hart Halt	ST205891
Up line railway bridge, Machen	ST210893
Down line railway bridge, Machen	ST210893
Machen West Junction	ST211893
Machen station and goods yard	ST211894
Machen Locomotive Works (site of)	ST217892
Church Road station	ST230883
Lower Machen railway bridge over A468	ST236878
Rhiwderin station	ST260874
Railway bridge near Rhiwderin station	ST260874
Bassaleg station	ST277872
Viaduct over River Ebbw near Bassaleg station	ST278872
Railway bridge over A467	ST282872

Great Western Railway

Bassaleg Junction, GWR	ST285868
Park Junction, GWR	ST296863

Park Mile, traceable from	ST286867	Rolling Bridge Junction	ST323852
	to ST294862	ANDR Company headquarters	ST319856
Gaer Tunnel (Park Junction end)	ST299866	Pill engine shed	ST312862
	to ST302868	Timber Float (site of)	ST311855
Monmouthshire Bank Sidings	ST304868		to ST314851
	to ST309864	North Lock (site of)	ST319856
West Mendalgief Junction	ST305864		to ST318855
Maesglas Junction (High Level)	ST303868	North Lock	ST314860
Alexandra Dock Junction	ST302867		to ST310854
Gaer Tunnel (Newport station end)	ST304873	Baileys Dry Dock	ST320854
	to ST306879		to ST318854
Newport High Street station	ST309883	1st South Lock (later East Lock)	ST322851
			to ST323852

ANDR internal dock lines and locks

		2nd South Lock (present entrance)	ST316843
East Mendalgief Junction	ST300864		to ST317837
Marshalling Sidings	ST311859	South Dock	ST318853
	to ST316851		to ST325849
Middle Connection (Junction Cut)	ST318853		to ST314842

ACKNOWLEDGEMENTS

To all those people that shared a moment of their time with me:

Those staff and management of the Associated British Ports Group of Newport and Cardiff that I have had the pleasure of meeting over many years, some still in office and some now retired: Mr R. C. F. Williams, Port Manager, Newport (now retired); Mr Haydon Jones, now retired, ABP, Newport; Mr Tony Williams, for his help, ABP, Newport; Mr Roy Burrows, also for his help, ABP, Newport; Mr Ray Stanbury, now retired, ABP, Cardiff; Mr Kevin Francis and Mr John Phelps, for their help, ABP, Cardiff.

I am also grateful to Mr Doug Jones of Associated British Ports, Cardiff, former Public Relations Officer, now also retired, for his help and the use of the Syren and Shipping magazine, edition of 1904, and for the use of the photographs and the information contained within, which over a period of time could be lost for ever.

I should also like to thank the following:

Aberdare Public Library and staff; Avon Anglia Publications, Weston Super Mare, and Mr G. Body.

Mrs E. Bartlett, Maesglas, Newport; Mr M. C. Bird, Whitchurch, Cardiff, for his help with the coloured postcards; Mr T. Bishop, Devon & Dorset Regimental Museum, Dorchester; Mr N. L. Browne, Surrey; Brown & Lenox Company, Pontypridd, especially to Mrs Griffiths, Personnel Manager.

Cardiff Public Library and staff, for permission to use photographs and information from their ANDR booklet of 1907; Mr R. M. Casserley, Berkhamsted; Mr Ray Caston, Newport, for his help and expertise on these docks; Mr T. D. Chapman, Radyr; Mr. Collins, Devon & Dorset Regimental Museum, Dorchester; Mr R. A. Cook, Oxfordshire; Mr John Cornwall, Bristol.

Mr J. J. Davis, Torquay, Devon; Mr Ken Davies, Hanson Quarries, Machen; Mr J. Dore Dennis, Westra.

Mr Martin Farquhar, Portland, Dorset: Mr David Fletcher, Librarian, Bovington Tank Museum, Dorset.

Great Western Railway Museum, Swindon, especially to the Curator, Mr Tim Bryan; Great Western Railway Staff Association Club, Newport, to the staff and members; Great Western Society, Didcot.

Mr V. C. Hardacre, Cardiff; Mr Cliff Harris, Porth, Rhondda, for his help and notes on the PCN line and these docks; Mr F. T. Hornby, Surrey.

Mr James, Forge and Hammer public house, White Hart, Machen; Mr and Mrs Jenkins, Machen; Mr D. K. Jones, Mountain Ash; Dr Stuart Owen Jones, Curator, Welsh Industrial and Maritime Museum, Cardiff; Mr Tony Jukes, for the loan of his photographs and the GWR booklet of 1934.

Mr C. Leigh, editor of Steam World, for the use of his notes on the Barnum & Bailey coaches taken from Model Railway Constructor, October 1983; Lens of Sutton, Surrey; Locomotive Club of Great Britain; Mr S. Meredith, Newport.

Mr B. J. Miller, Barry, S Glam; Mr Barrie Morris, Merthyr Tydfil, for his help, and also to all members of the Great Western Railway Staff Association at Merthyr, especially to Mr Mel Davies.

Newport Borough Council; Newport Public Library and staff, especially to Mr C. Graves and Mrs S. Pugh, Librarian; Newport Resource Centre and staff.

Oakwood Press, Headington, Oxford; Ordnance Survey Department, Southampton; Mr Graham Oxlande, Tonyrefail, Rhondda; Mr Huw Parry, Countryside Planning Dept, Pontypridd.

Mrs Parsons, Mendalgief, Newport; Pontypridd Observer newspaper and staff; Pontypridd Public Library, especially to Mr Adrian Burton and Mrs Penny Pugh for their help during my research; Mr Alun Powell, Rhydyfelin, for his helpful knowledge and his friendship over the years, also to his good wife Val, for putting up with me; Mr D. Rees, Pontypridd.

The Railway Magazine, especially the Editor, for permission to use excerpts and photographs from Vol 32 (1913), Vol 38 (1916), Vol 43 (1918), Vol 50 (1922), Vol 59 (1926); Mr Sid Rickard, Bishopbriggs, Glasgow; Mr D. J. Rees, Ynysybwl.

Mr I. Savage, Devon & Dorset Regimental Museum, Dorchester; Mr David Sims, for the loan of the ANDR booklets of 1904, 1914, 1916, and for the hospitality shown in the Newport Harbour Commissioners Office; South Glamorgan Libraries; Mr D. Spargo, Machen; Mr J. Stacey, Newport; Starling Press Publications, Risca.

Mr D. G. Thomas, London; Mr J. B. True, Oxford, owner of Trojan.

Westrail Enterprises, Westra; Mr Alun Wetheridge, Great Western Railway Staff Association, Newport; staff of the Welsh Industrial and Maritime Museum, Cardiff, especially Mr G. Hayward; Welsh Railway Research Circle members; Mr R. Wilding, Pontypridd; Mr Clive Williams, Countryside Planning Dept, Pontypridd; Mr I. L. Wright, Cambridge.

My gratitude also to the widow of the late Mr C. R. Clinker and the publishers Avon Anglia, who gave permission to use the notes from his register of closed halts and stations; to the memory of the late Mr T. B. Sands of Cardiff, and to the late Mr H. C. Casserley, of Berkhamsted, who did much to record on film the now vanished scenes of the South Wales railways; to Mr A. Merchant, for permission to include the sketch of White Hart Halt drawn by the late Mr W. Merchant; to His Honour Judge D. Watkin Powell, for his permission to use his late father's photographs of 1910, when he was Chief Draughtsman for the ANDR (these photographs are now on permanent loan to the WIMM, Cardiff; it is due to the foresight of this gentleman and others like him that such photographic records of the ANDR system have remained intact over the years); to the memory of the late Arthur Wallis of Newport, a very knowledgeable man; and lastly to the many railway enthusiasts who spend their time undertaking the task of restoration, the rebuilding of our past, so that the youngsters of today will find some interest and learning from their endeavours.

INDEX